Woman's Mission ...

Anonymous

WOMAN'S MISSION.

"L'ignorance où les femmes sont de leurs devoirs, l'abus qu'elles font de leur puissance, leur font perdre le plus beau et le plus précieux de leurs avantages, celui d'être utiles."—Madame Bernier.

THIRD AMERICAN EDITION.

NEW-YORK:

PUBLISHED BY WILEY AND PUTNAM,
No. 161 Broadway.

(J. P. WRIGHT, PRINTER, 18 NEW STREET.)

1841.

"What is wanting," said Napoleon, "that the youth of France be well educated?" "MOTHERS," replied Madame Campan. This reply struck the Emperor. "*Here*," said he, "*is a system of education in one word.* Be it your care to train up mothers who shall know how to educate their children."

AIMÉ MARTIN.

INTRODUCTORY LETTER,

TO THE YOUNG LADIES WHO ARE MEMBERS OF

ST. MARY'S HALL.

MY DAUGHTERS,

You can scarcely be expected to realize the amount of care and solicitude which my relation to you involves. When I take you from your parents, I feel that I assume the parental responsibilities ; and it is my effort and prayer so to discharge them, as I would expect, at the hands of another, towards daughters of mine. But great as the care and solicitude have been, which my relation to you has involved, I am happy in being able to say, that they have been far exceeded by the satisfaction of our intercourse. I thank GOD, that I can now say, that my highest aim has been obtained, in the establishment of St. Mary's Hall, upon a religious basis, and its government by a religious influence. The experience of the last year has demonstrated to my perfect and entire conviction, that our Christian household can be administered upon Christian principles ; and I look back to the administration, to thirty-one of your number, of the Apostolic ordinance of Confirmation, and to the admission of more than forty of you to the Lord's Supper, as among the happiest results of my whole ministry. God grant that upon a spring so fair, no blight may fall ! God grant that the buds of so much promise may ripen into golden and immortal fruit !

My daughters, I have never hesitated to avow, that my interest in the institution in whose bosom you are nurtured, is mainly founded on the natural and peculiar influence of your sex; and that my highest hope of it is as A SCHOOL FOR CHRIS TIAN MOTHERS. With what unmingled pleasure, under these circumstances, did I read, and read again, a second time, and a third time, the little volume which I now introduce to your acquaintance. It seemed thrown providentially in my way, to strengthen my hands and encourage my heart in the work which I had undertaken. It carries out and sustains, as I could not have done, the conceptions which were struggling in my bosom, of your high destiny and great responsibilities. It is the very book, which, if I had a thousand daughters, I would put into their hands, with the Bible and the Book of Common Prayer, as their best companion; and invaluable, as supplying at once the radiant chart of their career, and the inspiring motives to pursue it with untiring zeal and with unsparing self devotion. It is indeed a wonderful book. Seldom have I been so deeply affected as by its perusal. I feel that in procuring its publication, I am promoting, through the elevation of your sex the best and highest interests of the country; and I fervently invoke on its clear arguments and eloquent appeals, the blessing of the Holy One. I will detain you no longer, my dear daughters, from its perusal and companionship, than to subscribe myself, with deepest interest in your welfare, and devout commendation of you all to the Keeper of Israel,

Your affectionate Pastor and Parent in Christ,

G. W. DOANE.

St. Mary's Hall, Festival of All Saints, 1839.

PREFACE.

THE subject of the following pages has long engrossed my most serious thought. The result of this thought has produced the fullest conviction, that, if women could once be made to understand their real mission in this world, and to feel their own importance and responsibility, a surprising change must immediately take place in society, giving to it a higher tone and a purer spirit.

The work of M. Aimé Martin, *Sur l'Education des Mères*, &c., is eminently qualified to awaken attention to this subject, and to teach the true nature of our high calling. It is, therefore, matter of surprise and regret, that his excellent book should be so little read and appreciated in this country.

Wishing to make it better known to English women, it was my intention to translate M. Martin's work, and to adapt it as far as possible to the

1*

English taste. In pursuing this task, however, I found that a mere translation could not do sufficient justice to his eloquent spirit, and that the greater part of his work would not perhaps have much interest in an English dress. Many of his chapters are so exclusively addressed to the French nation, with respect to morals and manners, that his observations would lose much of their effect in this country, because not immediately applicable to English society. In dwelling upon his *particular* application of the fundamental principles upon which he insists, the reader might perhaps fail to discover that these were of *universal* application, equally sound and true, in all ages and in all countries.

Thus the work would, in a translation, lose much of its usefulness, as well as of its beauty. The nationality of M. Martin's work has, therefore, obliged me, most reluctantly, to abandon the design of intoducing it fully to the admiration of the English reader. At the same time I have been unwilling to relinquish the hope of rousing attention to this important subject, and since the attempt could not be made, as was first intended, *in the translation* of the thoughts of another, I have ventured to embody those ideas which have always occupied my own mind with engrossing interest. The following work is then the result of deep meditation on a long cherished subject. May its power of convincing be in some sort commensurate with the importance of its object.

In a few parts, more especially in Chapters II., IV., and VIII., passages have been adapted from M. Martin's work. Whenever this has been done, the translation is clearly distinguished from the original matter, by being enclosed in brackets, thus, [ ]. It is hoped that these few specimens will induce the reader to turn to the French work itself; it is impossible that any translation can adequately convey the beautiful spirit of the original.

CONTENTS.

———

		Page
INTRODUCTORY CHAPTER	. . . .	11
CHAPTER I. On Power and Influence	. . . .	14
" II. The Principle of Social Regeneration wanting	16
" III. Maternal Influence	22
" IV. The Influence of Women on Society .	37
" V. Proper Sphere for the Influence of Women.— Nature and Extent	47
" VI. On the Education of Women . .	54
" VII. Education, continued.—Love.—Marriage	67
" VIII. Maternal Love	81
" IX. The Nature of Influence.—Its Source	91
" X. The Influence of Personal Character .	94
" XI. On the Means of securing Personal Influence	101
" XII. The preceding Chapter, continued .	112
" XIII. Missionary Spirit	119
" XIV. Religion	127
Conclusion	147

I saw her upon nearer view,
A Spirit, yet a Woman too!
Her household motions light and free,
And steps of virgin liberty;
A countenance in which did meet
Sweet records, promises as sweet;
A creature not too bright or good
For human nature's daily food;
For transient sorrows, simple wiles,
Praise, blame, love, kisses, tears, and smiles.

And now I see, with eye serene,
The very pulse of the machine;
A being, breathing thoughtful breath,
A traveller betwixt life and death;
The reason firm, the temperate will,
Endurance, foresight, strength, and skill,
A PERFECT WOMAN, NOBLY PLANNED,
To warn, to comfort, and command;
And yet a Spirit still, and bright
With something of an Angel light.

WORDSWORTH.

WOMAN'S MISSION.

INTRODUCTORY CHAPTER.

.... Spirits are not finely touched,
But to fine issues.

SHAKSPEARE.

THE age in which we live is pre-eminently one of
novelty,—new plans, new discoveries, new truths,
new opinions, at least, whether true or chimerical.
Some of these relate to the position, political and
social, of woman, whose importance in the scale
of humanity, no rational being, above all, no Christian, can doubt. The " last at the Cross, and ear-
liest at the grave,"* are dignified in the eyes of all
Christian believers by the noble qualities of un-
worldliness and self-devotion ; and it is one among
many of the internal and collateral evidences of
Christianity, that its historians have so beautifully
and faithfully portrayed the distinction between
man's and woman's devotedness.

That the sex, characterized by such noble moral

[* Barrett's " Woman; a Poem."]

development, is destined to exercise no unimportant influence on the political and social condition
of mankind, we must all believe; indeed, the united
testimony of ages leaves this an undoubted fact.
There is a popular cry raised of injustice and oppression on the part of the other sex.   Yet men,
in all ages, have shown a sufficient willingness to
allow woman a share of influence, sometimes a
very undue share.   There is no hyperbole in the
phrase, " Vainqueurs des vainqueurs de la terre ;"
and this influence is so powerful, and so generally
felt, that it becomes a question whether it is used
as it ought to be,—for good.

But, it is said, it is degrading to work by influence, instead of by power,—indirectly, instead of
directly,—as subordinates, not as principals. Here
is the question at issue. Would mankind be benefitted by the exchange of influence for power, in
the case of woman? Would the greatest possible
good be procured by bringing her out of her present sphere into the arena of public life, by intro-
ducing to our homes and to our hearths the violent
dissensions, the hard and rancorous feelings, engendered by political strife?   It is really difficult
to approach the subject in the form to which it has
by some writers been reduced, with any degree of
gravity ; and it is somewhat to the credit of the
other sex, that it has not more frequently been
treated with the keen and indelicate satire which

it deserves, and might provoke. Yet we are not one iota behind these fiery champions of womanhood, in exalted notions of its dignity and mission. We are as anxious as they can be, that women should be roused to a sense of their own importance ; but we affirm, that it is not so much social institutions that are wanting to women, as women who are wanting to themselves. We claim for them no less an office than that of instruments (under God)* for the regeneration of the world,— restorers of God's image in the human soul. Can any of the warmest advocates of the political rights of woman claim or exert for her a more exalted mission,—a nobler destiny ! That she will best accomplish this mission by moving in the sphere which God and nature have appointed, and not by quitting that sphere for another, it is the object of these pages to prove.

[* The constant reference to the Divine blessing as the source of female influence, and to the Holy Spirit as inspiring and directing " Woman's Mission," and crowning it with due success, is what renders this a most attractive, not only, but most practicable book.]

2

CHAPTER I.

ON POWER AND INFLUENCE.

Power o'er the will exerts its iron sway,
While Influence gently lures us on our way.—*

THERE are two principles by which men act upon the minds of their fellow-men, viz: power and influence. Power is principally exerted in the shape of authority, and is limited in its sphere of action. Influence has its source in human sympathy, and is as boundless in its operation.

If there were any doubt which of these principles most contributes to the formation of human character, we have only to look around us. We see that power, while it regulates men's actions, cannot reach their opinions. It cannot modify dispositions nor implant sentiments, nor alter character. All these things are the work of influence. Men frequently resist power, while they yield to influence an unconscious acquiescence.

What is it that occasions the varied mental physiognomy of the different tribes of the human race? What (except a slight hereditary difference of form *and colour*) distinguish the infant heir of an English duke and the infant burden of an Indian squaw? Let us suppose it possible for them to exchange positions; the child of the red hunter will grow up with all the feelings of an European aristocrat,—the ducal heir with those of a wild red man. To what is this owing? To systematic endeavours on the part of others to give a current to the thoughts? No! to those nameless and undefinable influences which different social institutions exercise upon their members. And if we extend our speculations into every possible ramification of society, the same result follows. Even Christianity itself has achieved, and is to achieve, its greatest triumphs, not by express commands or prohibitions, but by a thousand indirect influences, emanating from its spirit rather than its letter. From the above facts, two deductions seem necessarily to follow.

1st. That the possessors of influence are awfully responsible for its use.

2d. That to the misunderstanding or misdirecting of influences may, in a great measure, be attributed the slow progress of mankind in the moral regeneration* of their race, as compared with their intellectual advancement.

[* Though this may be the most suitable, it is not an adequate expression. Regeneration is but the commencement of that change from whose progress towards perfection such excellent *results are* looked for.]

CHAPTER II.

THE PRINCIPLE OF SOCIAL REGENERATION WANTING.

Tous ces honneurs mondains ne sont qu'un bien sterile,
Des humaines vertus recompense fragile,
Un dangereux éclat qui passe et qui s'enfuit,
Que le trouble accompagne et que la mort detruit.

VOLTAIRE.

It has been asserted that the moral progress of our race does not keep pace with the intellectual; and it has been assumed that one of the chief causes of this slow progress is the misdirecting of influence, and expecting power to supply the want, and perform the work, of influence. The fact has not escaped the acuteness of philanthropists; the true remedy appears to have done so. They have attributed the evil to the errors of political institutions, and to the absence of intellectual culture: the amelioration of these evils affords only partial remedies for one more remote. An error in first principles can be rectified by no after-application of scientific rules. In vain does the cultivator lavish his pains on the plant which has the canker *at its root*; he may, indeed, produce a show of leaves and blossoms, but the seat of vitality is poisoned : it perishes in spite of his care.

Political theorists expect moral results from the amendment of political institutions ; whereas it is obvious that such improvements are the effect, and not the cause, of the moral progress of the governed. Men must have virtue enough to desire good institutions before they will exert themselves to attain them. It is not denied that good institutions (so desired and obtained) are beneficial; but as a reaction, not as a primary agent. The attempt to force good institutions on men unable to appreciate their value, produces effects not advantageous, but highly injurious.

, Political economists expect moral results from external prosperity: confounding prosperity with happiness, and thinking that happiness induces goodness, they labour to remove obstacles to external prosperity. It is right, it is benevolent, so to do ; and good results follow, but the results which they expect will not follow. They have taken up a false position. ["When society takes for its ultimate object the physical well-being of the community, it makes men active, ardent, restless, enemies of each other, insatiable in the pursuit of riches and pleasure,—not better, or happier."*]

That the principle of moral regeneration is not

---

* Aimé Martin.

2*

in external prosperity, we have proof in a country the political position and institutions of which allow her to make (as much as it is possible for any government to do) ample provision for the temporal wants of the government. Is the aggregate of happiness increased? Does the cry of sinning and suffering humanity rise less loudly to heaven? The friends of instruction look upon intellectual culture as the grand panacea for all evils; and the enlightened and benevolent exhaust themselves in efforts to extend to the many the advantages once confined to the few. Good results follow, but not the results expected. Intellectual by no means involves moral progress,—this we see in nations: intellectual by no means involves moral superiority,—this we see, alas! in gifted individuals. Our history, past and contemporary, holds up to us two most striking examples of this truth,—Bacon and Byron; those splendid intelligences who both disgraced the godlike gifts bestowed upon them: and the errors of each were of a kind, against which, if against any, intellectual superiority might be supposed to afford a safeguard. Bacon's sordid avarice, and Byron's grovelling sensuality, are vices not even of that kind, the daring criminality of which gives an impression almost of the sublime. No one will imagine that their superiority of intellect is charged with having produced these faults; *but we are fairly* entitled to deduce that, though intellect may give dignity and vigour to moral sentiments where they do exist, it has no tendency to produce them where they do not. Nay, like an unprincipled ally, it is ever ready to aid either party, and to lend energy to bad passions, as well as loftiness to good ones. It is a singular corroborating fact, that the grosser passions are never found in co-existence with the higher moral sentiments; such co-existence being not only possible, but frequent in the case of intellect.

[" We are now to develope our grand principle. We see that it is in vain to seek in political institutions, or intellectual cultivation, the moral regeneration of the world. It is neither industry, nor science, nor machinery, nor books, which can make the happiness of a people. All these things are useful in their places, and it ought to be the care of the legislator to multiply them; but if, content with having developed the intellect, that earthly part of man, he neglects the soul, that emanation from the Divinity, he will only see around him a multitude, restless through unbridled passions, tormented by the desire of aggrandizement and the thirst of knowledge. These instincts, in themselves sublime, become a torment. They have been directed to the earth, and remain there, grovelling in the midst of riches and pleasures. Why have you not opened to them the way to heaven? All that gives repose to the heart, all that really elevates humanity, comes from above. The most intellectual, if they be not at the same time the most religious people, will never be the sovereign people."*]

We see, then, how men may be rendered better and happier; in other words, on what principles depend the regeneration of mankind: on the cultivation of the religious and moral portion of their nature, which cultivation no government has yet attempted; over which, in fact, governments and public institutions have little or no control. It is in the cultivation of that divine spirit of unselfish rectitude, which has love for its origin, and the good of others for its aim; a spirit opposed—oh how opposed!—to the selfish and grovelling utilitarianism which it appears to be the unfortunate tendency of physical improvements to promote and which intellectual culture at best serves but to neutralize. Principles have their chief source in influences :—early influences, above all; and early influences have more power in forming character than institutions or mental cultivation; it is therefore to the arbiters of these that we must look for the regenerating principle. We must seek, then some fundamental principle, some spirit indefatigable, delighting in its task, and which may pervade the whole of society. Such a principle we

* Aimé Martin.

find in family affection,—especially in maternal affection. Have we, then, been too bold in asserting that women may be the prime agents of God in the regeneration of mankind?

["Napoleon said one day to Madame Campan: 'The old systems of instruction are worth nothing. What is wanting, in order that the youth of France be well educated?' 'Mothers!' replied Madame Campan. This reply struck the Emperor. 'Here,' said he, 'is a system of education in one word. Be it your care to train up mothers who shall know how to educate their children.' This profound remark is the very subject of our book; it contains, perhaps, the secret of a mighty regeneration."*]

* Aimé Martin.

CHAPTER III.

MATERNAL INFLUENCE.

All originates in the mysterious workings of a mother's heart.—LINDSAY.

["THE moral destinies of the world, then, depend not so much upon institutions, or upon education, as upon moral influence. The most powerful of all moral influences is the maternal. On the maternal character depends the mind, the prejudices, the virtues of nations; in other words, the regeneration of mankind. Are, then, the claims made for women in these pages too exalted? Is it not one of the most important services that can be rendered to mankind, to impress upon their minds the fact of this influence, and to enlighten them as to its nature and extent? It appears as though Nature had expressly co-ordained the relation of mother and child with a view to this influence. With what care has she formed the sympathies that unite them,—beauty, grace, gaiety, and, above all, the affections of the heart! Curiosity is met by patience; petulance by mildness; the ignorance of *the child* is never humiliated by pedantry in the mother, so completely is intellectual superiority chastened by love. In a word, the very qualities which it has been customary to reproach as weaknesses, the flexibility, the love of the marvellous, the power of being occupied by trifles, which are sometimes regarded as feminine defects, seem destined still more closely to unite the two souls thus formed for each other. The silver links which twine around them both, unite them in the closest union.

"It is of the utmost consequence to remark, that in children sentiment precedes intelligence; the first answer to the maternal smile is the first dawn of intelligence; the first sensation is the responding caress. Comprehension begins in feeling; hence, to her who first arouses the feelings, who first awakens the tenderness, must belong the happiest influences. She is not, however, to teach virtue, but to inspire it. This is peculiarly the province of woman. What she wishes us to be, she begins by making us love, and love begets unconscious imitation. What is a child in relation to a tutor? An ignorant being whom he is called upon to instruct. What is a child in relation to a mother? An immortal being, whose soul it is her business to train for immortality. Good schoolmasters make good scholars—good mothers make good men: here is the difference of their missions. It follows, that the education, properly so called of the child, depends almost entirely on mothers, and if they have been too willing to trust to delegated authority for its accomplishment, it is because they have identified education with instruction, two things essentially different, and which it is essential to separate; for instruction may be interrupted, and pass from hand to hand, but education should be of one piece; whatever interrupts it, hinders it—whoever abandons it after having undertaken it, may see her child lost in the wanderings of error, or, what is more deplorable, in utter indifference to virtue.

" If an instructor can, without effort, descend to the comprehension of a pupil; if he can form a religious heart, a man of integrity, he has done all that is required of him. And what is there in all this, of which a woman is incapable? Who better than a mother can teach us to prefer honour to riches—to love our fellow-creatures—to raise our souls to the only source of goodness and infinitude. A common tutor counsels and moralizes what he commits to our memory; a mother engraves on our heart; she makes us love what he only makes us believe; it is through love that we arrive at virtue. Will it be said that high political interests demand more enlightened interpreters?"*]
The political interests, inseparable from the moral

* Aimé Martin.

interests of mankind, do not depend upon the basis of learning, but of conscience, for their foundation. Learning is only so far valuable as it tends to enlighten and enlarge the views of conscience. Who so fit to lay this foundation as woman, who, to the enlarged capacity of the other sex, should add the uncompromising fidelity, the unselfish devotedness of her own?

["This maternal influence exists everywhere; in the cabin of the poor, as in the palace of the rich. Everywhere it determines our sentiments, our opinions, and our tastes. 'The fate of a child,' said Napoleon, 'is always the work of his mother;' and this extraordinary man took pleasure in repeating, that to his mother he owed his elevation. All history confirms this opinion."*]

* I cannot do justice, in a translation, to the following eloquent passage from Aimé Martin, and therefore give it in the original:—"L'histoire est là pour justifier ces paroles; et sans nous appuyer des exemples si mémorables de Charles IX. et de Henri IV., de l'élève de Catherine de Medicis et de l'élève de Jeanne d'Albret, Louis XIII. ne fut-il pas, comme sa mère, faible, ingrat et malheureux, toujours révolté et toujours soumis! Ne reconnaissez-vous pas dans Louis XIV. les passions d'une femme Espagnole, ces galanteries tout à la fois sensuelles et romanesques, ces terreurs de dévot, cet orgueil de despote qui veut qu'on se prosterne devant le trône comme devant l'autel? On a dit, et je le crois, que la femme qui donna le jour aux deux Corneille avait l'âme grande, l'esprit élevé, les mœurs sévères, qu'elle ressemblait à la mère des Gracques, que c'étaient deux femmes de même étoffe. Au rebours, la mère du jeune Arouet,

The fate of society is more particularly affected by this power, because it is more especially influ- ential on the character of men. Most great men have had extraordinary mothers, and it seems, as though by some peculiar influence, the nature o the mother acts upon the son. It may be really so but if this doctrine be objected to as fanciful, le us try to account for it in a more philosophica manner. It is as notorious as it is unfortunate that the maternal influence is almost the only moral influence to which boys in their early train ing are subjected. In the education of girls, no one would dare to assume that absolute indiffer ence to moral results,* which has been not only permitted, but authorized in the instructors of boys Neither are they to be blamed, for, provided the power of conveying the requisite instruction in Latin and Greek was proved, who ever inquired into the capabilities of a schoolmaster as a mora trainer of youth? Nay, most persons entered on the office without the slightest notion that they

railleuse, spirituelle, coquette et galante, marqua de tous ce traits le génie de son fils; elle anima ces cent âmes de ce fe violent qui devait à la fois éclairer et consumer, produire tan de chefs-d'œuvre, et se déshonorer par tant de facéties!" [Th venerable Bishop White ascribed to the influence of his mother instructions the impressions of piety and virtue which directe him through life, and consoled his death.]

[* I would that this were more strictly true.]

were expected to be such. The idea is quite a novel one! so novel, that even now it is most difficult for conscientious parents to find a school in which the moral and religious training of boys is not left at an awful distance behind the intellectual. The *origin* of this error must ever be involved in obscurity; at least, until it can be proved that men on entering life are subject to fewer temptations, or possessed of greater power to resist them, than women. The *results*, unfortunately, labour under no difficulty on the score of obscurity, and are such that it does not become a woman's pen to make other than a passing allusion to them.

But even those who do take some heed to preserve boys from the contaminating influence, which makes them an easy prey to flagrant immorality, seem to have no conception that it is their place to watch over the minor points of character, which, though they may not affect a man's good fame, and hinder his worldly advancement, materially influence his happiness and his virtue. The regulation of temper, the repression of selfishness, the examination of motive—how seldom do they form any part of the training of boys! The neglect has a most fatal effect on their happiness, and the happiness of all connected with them. We may see it illustrated in that curious popular paradox, which allows a man to be by his unregulated temper the torment of all around him, and yet retain the name of a "thoroughly good-hearted fellow."—How far the "good heart" brings forth good fruits, may be read in the anxious looks of the timid wife—the unchild-like and joyless manners of frightened children—the obsequious but unloving obedience of domestics—all fearing to awake the lion's wrath. A woman with such a temper is deservedly called a vixen, but a man is "a good-hearted fellow." Except it can be proved that there is a different moral code for the two sexes, it is very puzzling to simple-minded people to know why that which excites merited dislike in a woman, is so leniently passed over in a man: nay, of the two, we should say that the ill temper of a man has less excuse than that of a woman, because he has more power to escape from domestic annoyances.   The error here is in the fundamental principle, which makes the regulation of temper no part of the education of boys; such neglect is the greatest possible cruelty, for it adds tenfold difficulty to that internal conflict which all must sustain, who are anxious to improve their own character. Violence of temper is so easily corrected in early childhood, that judicious early training may almost always save this trouble in after-years.

Again, men are said to be more selfish than women.   How can they help it? no pains are taken in their education to make them otherwise.   That *pugnacity* which is so admired as a proof of *spirit,* is the very embodiment of the selfish principle—a fighting for their *own* rights—an assertion of their *own* superiority. They are taught at school to despise the weak, and practise the lesson at home in petty domestic torments to the weak of their circle—their sisters; receiving, at the same time, from those very sisters, a thousand little services, without consciousness and without gratitude. Is it astonishing that these boys should hereafter be selfish husbands and tyrannical fathers? Considering how little the moral training of boys has, (even in profession,) formed a part of their education, the only subject of astonishment is, that any should escape the evil effect of such a system, and not that many fall victims to it.

A reflecting mind will have no difficulty in ackowledging the bearing of these well-known facts upon the points under discussion, viz: the importance of maternal influence on the character of boys. As there is a great chance that, except they receive religious and moral principles from their mothers, their whole life may pass without any attempt to impress them with such,—does it not become of unspeakable importance, that they be detained as long as possible under maternal influence? Yet the very contrary is usually the case, and boys are removed even sooner than girls from the beneficial atmosphere of purity and love, with which family affection, and, above all, ma-

3*

ternal affection, environs them. And then men are
blamed as cold, and hard, and selfish! It would
be as natural to feel surprise, that the plant exposed to the constant action of a petrifying spring
loses its vegetable characteristics, and turns to
stone. Till the intellectual will condescend to
become likewise the moral trainers of youth, let
them imbibe as long as possible that pure and beneficent influence which may be their soul's preservative in the midst of moral danger. Dr. John-
son said, with his usual acuteness, that " except a
man have received some early tincture of piety,
he no more knows how to set about being religious, than a man who has never learned figures,
can count when he has need of calculation;" and
it is a remarkable fact, that men, who, after long
wandering in the paths of error, have found a
way of return to religion and virtue, are generally able to refer to some early recollections of les-
sons implanted by a pious mother.

Oh, why are mothers in such haste to delegate
to others the delightful task which Providence has
assigned to them? Why do they hasten to intrust
the unformed mind—the unsettled principles of
their sons to the ungenial influence of scholastic
establishments? Do they thereby hope to lessen
the weighty sense of responsibility? It is a vain
hope. They, as the guardian angels of man's
infancy, are charged with a mission—to them is

committed the implanting that heavenly germ to which God must indeed give the increase : but for the early culture of which they are answerable. The importance of early impressions—of *home* impressions—is proved by the extreme difficulty of eradicating or counteracting them, if bad. Conscientious teachers of youth can bear ample testimony to this fact. They have often occasion to lament, with grief and humiliation, the powerlessness of their most devoted endeavours to remove early bad impressions—or to do anything more than just palliate the effects of unfavourable domestic influences—of an unhealthy domestic atmosphere. It is the mother who, as the source of moral influence, is the former of the moral atmosphere. The reason of this fact will be the subject of a future inquiry: in the mean time, I shall take the liberty of assuming it as a fact, and of entreating mothers to attend to it. What should we think of parents who should voluntarily shut up their children in the ward of a fever hospital? Our first impulse would be to convey them to Bedlam. Yet no such sensation arises on beholding the corrupted nature of that moral atmosphere, on which depends the life of their souls—of those souls which will one day be required of them at the bar of God ! *Moral* contagion is more dangerous than physical, by far. Would that the horror with which the one is regarded could be, in any de-

gree, extended to the other! It is difficult t<
press, it would be almost impossible to mak<
ignorant and unobservant believe, the pow<
indirect influences over the minds of chil<
These indirect influences are their moral a
sphere. Try to win the affections of a chil<
gifts, by personal caresses, by flattery, it turns
you with indifference. You wonder at its ing
tude. Do you wish to know the cause? It
the harsh word, the unjust deed towards ano
that neutralized your efforts at gaining affec
Talk to an older child on the folly and sinfu
of vanity, the worthlessness of worldly dis
tions—you find the seeds of vanity and amb
springing up in her heart, and tax your mer
for the cause. It may perhaps be found in
own self-complacent glances at your mirror—
fonder kiss and brighter smile bestowed on o:
your children more gifted by Nature than the r<
your eager deferential reception of those of
acquaintance distinguished by worldly great
compared with that bestowed on less eminent <
"Deeds, not words," is the motto of all si
people, children included; and keenly do they
and deeply do they, by their future con
avenge, the substitution of words for deeds
shadows for substances.

It may be urged, that this notion of a r
atmosphere is chimerical. It is not. "We s

that we do know." It may also be said that even
if true, it is charging women with too weighty a
responsibility to attribute the power of its formation
to them, when counteracting influences so mightily
oppose the action of their minds. The counteracting influences may arise from two principal sources. 1st. The unhappiness of having an uncon-
genial partner in life, who, instead of seconding a
mother's efforts, thwarts, or is indifferent to them.
2d. The necessary intercourse with society which
subjects children to many influences besides the
parental. The former of these objections will be
met and treated in a subsequent chapter,—and for
the latter—the mother, who cannot meet and overcome it in the might and by the power of maternal
love, is not one of the mothers intended to be here
invoked as regenerators of mankind.

There is another particular in which the character of the mother greatly influences the views and
welfare of her sons, which ought to be treated of,
for it is not enough impressed upon the maternal
heart. It is of the utmost importance to the virtue
and happiness of men, that they enter life with
exalted notions of female character, and that they
be not satisfied with the semblance without the
reality of virtue. Let each mother then engrave
upon the heart of her son such an image of feminine virtue and loveliness, as may make it sufficient for him to turn his eyes inward in order to

draw thence a power sufficient to combat evil, ar
to preserve him from wretchedness. And here,
may observe, is a great inducement for mothers t
cultivate their intellectual powers, for those powe:
will materially affect their influence over grown-u
sons. Unintellectual mothers of gentle temper
good sense, and strict moral principle, may be, ar
often are, most excellent trainers of childhood
but it is important, that as sons emerge from chil(
hood, respect and veneration be added to fon(
ness. It is good that they should continue to loo
up.* It will be shown in a subsequent chapte
what an injurious effect the want of mental equal
ty produces on feminine influence. It has mo
powerfully and injuriously operated on society;
may operate as powerfully and injuriously in iı
dividual cases. Young men, flushed with tł
pride of intellect on entering life, are sometim(
impatient of control; fathers are often without ta(
to exercise wholesome authority in such a way ɛ
not to wound that pride: the check is then d(
posited in the mother's hands; *she* will have r.
want of tact in using it, for it is precisely in thɛ
delicate and indescribable application of means t
ends, called "tact," that women are proverbiall
skilled. This very power, however, presumes
certain degree of mental superiority, and the grea

[* *There is a world of wisdom in this little sentence.*]

er the superiority, the greater the power. The error, then, is a very lamentable one, into which some very conscientious women fall, who, on entering life, allow themselves to be so engrossed by present duties as to forget other and more important duties which the maturity of their children will entail upon them. They forget that, though they are mothers of infants now, they will be mothers of men and women by-and-bye. High moral principle and devoted maternal love will make them safe and efficient guides for childhood, but they will possibly have to be the guides of early manhood—and here intelligence must aid devotedness. Mothers are apt to forget that not to advance is to retrograde, and many give up in early married life all continuance of intellectual cultivation; these find in after-life, not only that they are inferior to what their duty and position require of them; but they often discover with grief and surprise that they are inferior to what they themselves were in their youth. The maternal influence, so valuable at all periods of life, and so especially valuable at this period, gradually loses its power; narrow views and sentiments hinder its operation; for the young have little indulgence for the frailties of others, though needing so much for their own. It is probably owing to this want of progression in the parental mind, that we often see laudable efforts deprived of their just reward. It is vain to produce age as a title to respect, if length of days have produced decrease, not increase of enlightenment. If the progress of the youthful mind, and the progress of society, be not met by a corresponding progress in the parental views and feelings, youth will turn to other and less safe advisers than their parents, and parents will thus, perhaps, lose the reward of a life of effort and exertion. The combination of high mental power with feminine purity and unselfishness gives a dignity to intellectual maternity which really overawes the youthful mind; and unless it be totally corrupt, has a great tendency to stamp it indelibly with virtuous sentiments, and with those high views of feminine character which are so essential to man's happiness and goodness. Upon these views depend, in a great measure, his choice of a companion in life, so that the character of the mother may often be said to influence the fate of the son long after she has ceased to exist. Her image, engraven on his heart in life, or speaking from the tomb in death, will still interpose itself between him and objects unworthy of his choice, as of her memory; and perhaps secure the son of her love from the misery and guilt which attachments to undeserving objects always entail upon their victims.

CHAPTER IV.

THE INFLUENCE OF WOMEN ON SOCIETY.

If aught of goodness or of grace
Be mine, *hers* be the glory ;
She led me on in wisdom's path,
And set the light before me.
PIERRE VIDAL, *Troubadour.*

"WHATEVER may be the customs and laws of a country, women always give the tone to morals. Whether slaves or free, they reign, because their empire is that of the affections.　This influence, however, is more or less salutary, according to the degree of esteem in which they are held :—they make men what they are.　It seems as though Nature had made man's intellect depend upon their dignity, as she has made his happiness depend upon their virtue.　This, then, is the law of eternal justice,—man cannot degrade woman without himself falling into degradation : he cannot elevate her without at the same time elevating himself. Let us cast our eyes over the globe !　Let us observe those two great divisions of the human race, the East and the West.　Half the old world re-

4

mains in a state of inanity, under the oppression
of a rude civilization: the women there are slaves;
the other advances in equalization and intelligence : the women there are free and honoured.

" If we wish, then, to know the political and
moral condition of a state, we must ask what
rank women hold in it. Their influence embraces the whole life. A wife,—a mother,—two
magical words, comprising the sweetest sources of
man's felicity. Theirs is the reign of beauty, of
love, of reason. Always a reign ! A man takes
counsel with his wife ; he obeys his mother ; he
obeys her long after she has ceased to live, and the
ideas which he has received from her become
principles stronger even than his passions.

" The reality of the power is not disputed ; but it
may be objected that it is confined in its operation
to the family circle : as if the aggregate of families
did not constitute the nation ! The man carries
with him to the forum the notions which the woman has discussed with him by the domestic
hearth. His strength there realizes what her gentle insinuations inspired. It is sometimes urged
as matter of complaint that the business of women
is confined to the domestic arrangements of the
household : and it is not recollected that from the
household of every citizen issue forth the errors
and prejudices which govern the world !

" *If, then*, there be an incontestable fact, it is the

influence of women : an influence extended, with various modifications, through the whole of life. Such being the case, the question arises, by what inconceivable negligence a power of universal operation has been overlooked by moralists, who, in their various plans for the amelioration of man- kind, have scarcely deigned to mention this potent agent. Yet evidence, historical and parallel, proves that such negligence has lost to mankind the most influential of all agencies. The fact of its existence cannot be disputed ; it is, therefore, of the greatest importance that its nature should be rightly understood, and that it be directed to right objects."*]

It would not be uninteresting to trace the action and re-action by which women have degraded and been degraded,—alternately the source and the victims of mistaken social principles ; but it would be foreign to the design and compass of this work to do so. The subject, indeed, would afford matter for a philosophical treatise of deep interest, rather than for a chapter of a small work. A rapid historical sketch, and a few deductions which seem to bear upon the main point, are all that can be here attempted.

The Gospel announced on this, as on every other subject, a grand comprehensive principle,

* Aimé Martin.

which it was to be the work of ages (perhaps of eternity) to develope. The rescue of this degraded half of the human race was henceforth the ascertained will of the Almighty. But a long series of years were to elapse before this will worked out its issues. Its decrees, with the noble doctrines of which it formed a part, lay buried beneath the ruins of human intellect. But they were only buried, not destroyed ; and rose, like wild flowers on a ruined edifice, to adorn the irregularity which they could not conceal. The fantastic institutions of chivalry which it is now the fashion to deride (how unjustly !) were among the first scions of this plant of heavenly origin. They bore the impress of heaven, faint and distorted indeed, but not to be mistaken ! Devotion to an ideal good,—self-sacrifice,—subjugation of selfish and sensual feelings ; wherever these principles are found, disguised, disfigured though they be, they are not of the earth,—earthly. They, like the fabled amaranth, are plants which are not indigenous here below ! The seeds must come from above, from the source of all that is pure, of all that is good ! Of these principles the Gospel was the remote source ; women were the disseminators. [" Shut up in their castellated towers, they civilized the warriors who despised their weakness, and rendered less barbarous the passions and prejudices which themselves shared."*] It was they who directed the savage passions and brute force of men to an unselfish aim, the defence of the weak, and added to courage the only virtue then recognized—humanity. ["Thus chivalry prepared the way for law, and civilization had its source in gallantry."†]

At this epoch the influence of women was decidedly beneficial; happy for them and for society if it had continued to be so! If we attempt to trace the source of this influence, we shall find it in the intellectual equality of the two sexes; equally ignorant of what we call knowledge, the respect due by men to virtue and beauty was not checked by any disdain of real or fancied superiority on their part.

The intellectual exercises (chiefly imaginative) of the time, so far from forming a barrier between the two sexes, were a bond of union. The song of the minstrel was devoted to the praise of beauty, and paid by her smile. The spirit of the age, as embodied in these effusions, is the best proof of the beneficial influence exercised over that age by our sex. In them the name of woman is not associated in the degrading catalogue of man's pleasures, with his bottle and his horse, but is coupled with all that is fair and pure in nature,—the fields, the

---

* Aime Martin. † Ibid.

birds, the flowers; or high in virtue or sentiment,
—with honour, glory, self-sacrifice.

To the age of chivalry succeeded the revival of
letters; and (strange to say!) this revival was any
thing but advantageous to the cause of women.
Men found other paths to glory than the exercise of
valour afforded, and paths into which women were.
forbidden to follow them. Into these newly-dis-
covered regions, women were not allowed to pene-
trate, and men returned thence with real or affected
contempt for their unintellectual companions, without having attained true wisdom enough to know
how much they would gain by their enlightenment.

The advance of intelligence in men not being
met by a corresponding advance in women, the
latter lost their equilibrium in the social balance.
Honour, glory, were no longer attached to the
smile of beauty. The dethroned sovereigns, from
being imperious, became abject, and sought, by
paltry arts, to perpetuate the empire which was no
longer conceded as a right. Influence they still
possessed, but an influence debased in its character, and changed in its mode of operation. Instead
of being the objects of devotion of heart,—fantastic, indeed, but high-minded,—they became the
mere playthings of the imagination, or worse, the
mere objects of sensual passion. Respect is the
only sure foundation of influence. Women had
ceased to be respected, they therefore ceased to be

beneficially influential. That they retained another and a worse kind of influence, may be inferred
from the spirit, as embodied in the literature of
the period. Fiction no longer sought its heroes
amongst the lofty in mind and pure in morals—
its heroines in spotless virgins and faithful wives.
The reckless voluptuary, the faithless and successful adulteress,—these were the noble beings whose
deeds filled the pages which formed the delight of
the wise and the fair. The ultimate issues of
these grievous errors were most strikingly developed in the respective courts of Louis XIV. and
Charles II., where they reached their climax. The
vicious influence of which we have spoken was
then at its height, and the degradation of women
had brought on its inevitable consequence, the degradation of men. With some few exceptions,
(such exceptions, indeed, prove rules!) we trace
this evil influence in the contempt of virtue, public
and private; in the base passions, the narrow and
selfish views peculiar to degraded women, and re-
flected on the equally degraded men whom such
women could have power to charm.*

A change of opinions and of social arrangements
has long been operating, which ought entirely to
have abrogated these evils. That they have not
done so is owing to a grand mistake. Women

* See the Memoirs of Pepys, Evelyn, De Grammont, &c.

having recovered their rights, moral and intellectual, have resumed their importance in the eye of reason: they have long been the ornaments of society, which from them derives its tone, and it has become too much the main object of their education to cultivate the accomplishments which may make them such. A two-fold injury has arisen from this mistaken aim; it has blinded women as to the true nature and end of their existence, and has excited a spirit of worldly ambition opposed to the devoted unselfishness necessary for its accomplishment. This is the error of the unthinking—the reflecting have fallen into another, but not less serious one. The coarse, but expressive satire of Luther, " That the human mind is like an intoxicated man on horseback,—if he is set up on one side, he falls off on the other," was never more fully justified than on this subject. Because it is perceived that women have a dignity and value greater than society or themselves have discovered,—because their talents and virtues place them on a footing of equality with men, it is maintained that their present sphere of action is too contracted a one, and that they ought to share in the public functions of the other sex. Equality, mental and *physical,* is proclaimed! This is matter too ludicrous to be treated anywhere but in a professed satire; in sober earnest, it may be asked, upon what *grounds so* extraordinary a doctrine is built up?

Were women allowed to act out these principles, it would soon appear that one great range of duty had been left unprovided for in the schemes of Providence; such an omission would be without parallel. Two principal points only can here be brought forward which oppose this plan at the very outset; they are—

1st. Placing the two sexes in the position of rivals, instead of coadjutors, entailing the diminution of female influence.

2d. Leaving the important duties of woman only in the hands of that part of the sex least able to perform them efficiently.

The principle of divided labour seems to be a maxim of the divine government, as regards the creature. It is only by a concentration of powers to one point, that so feeble a being as man can achieve great results. Why should we wish to set aside this salutary law, and disturb the beautiful simplicity of arrangement which has given to man the power, and to woman the influence, to second the plans of Almighty goodness? They are formed to be co-operators, not rivals, in this great work; and rivals they would undoubtedly become, if the same career of public ambition and the same rewards of success were open to both. Woman, at present, is the regulating power of the great social machine, retaining, through the very exclusion complained of, the power to judge of questions by the abstract rules of right and wrong—a power seldom possessed by those whose spirits are chafed by opposition, and heated by personal contest.

The second resulting evil is a grave one, though in treating of it, also, it is difficult to steer clear of ludicrous associations. The political career being open to women, it is natural to suppose that all the most gifted of the sex would press forward to confer upon their country the benefit of their services, and to reap for themselves the distinction which such services would obtain; the duties hitherto considered peculiar to the sex would sink to a still lower position in public estimation than they now hold, and would be abandoned to those least able conscientiously to fulfil them. The combination of legislative and maternal duties would indeed be a difficult task, and, of course, the least ostentatious would be sacrificed.

Yet women have a mission! aye, even a political mission of immense importance! which they will best fulfil by moving in the sphere assigned them by Providence: not comet-like, wandering in irregular orbits, dazzling indeed by their brilliancy, but terrifying by their eccentric movements and doubtful utility. That the sphere in which they are required to move is no mean one, and that its apparent contraction arises only from a defect of intellectual vision, it is the object of the succeeding *chapters to* prove.

CHAPTER V.

PROPER SPHERE FOR THE INFLUENCE OF WOMEN—NATURE AND EXTENT.

On home's high duties be your thoughts employed,
Leave to the world its strivings, and its void.—Σ.

" THE fact of this influence being proved, it is of the utmost importance that it be impressed upon the mind of women, and that they be enlightened as to its true nature and extent."

The task is as difficult as it is important, for it demands some exercise of sober judgment to view it with requisite impartiality; it requires, too, some courage to encounter the charge of inconsistency which a faithful discharge of it entails. For it *is* an apparent inconsistency to recommend at the same time expansion of views and contraction of operation; to awaken the sense of power, and to require that the exercise of it be limited; to apply at once the spur and the rein. That intellect is to be invigorated only to enlighten conscience—that conscience is to be enlightened only to act on details—that accomplishments and graces are to be cultivated only, or chiefly, to adorn obscurity;—a list of

somewhat paradoxical propositions indeed, and hard
to be received; yet, upon their favourable reception
depends, in my opinion, the usefulness of our influence, the destinies of our race, and it is my intention to direct all my observations to this point.

It is astonishing and humiliating to perceive how
frequently human wisdom, especially argumenta-
tive wisdom, is at fault as to results, while accident,
prejudices, or common sense, seem to light upon
truths which reason feels after without finding.   It
appears as though *à priori* reasoning, human nature being the subject, is like a skilful piece of me-
chanism, carefully and scientifically put together,
but which some perverse and occult trifle will not
permit to act.   This is eminently true of many
questions regarding education, and precisely the
state of the argument concerning the position and
duties of women. The facts of moral and intellectual equality being established, it seems somewhat
irrational to condemn women to obscurity and
detail for their field of exertion, while men usurp
the extended one of public usefulness.   And a
good case may be made out on this very point.
Yet the conclusions are false and pernicious, and
the prejudices which we now smile at as obsolete,
are truths of nature's own imparting, only wanting
the agency of comprehensive intelligence to make
them valuable, by adapting them to the present
state of society. For, as one atom of falsehood in

first principles nullifies a whole theory, so one principle, fundamentally true, suffices to obviate many minor errors. This fundamentally true principle, I am prepared to show, exists in the established opinions concerning the true sphere of women, and that, whether originally dictated by reason, or derived from a sort of intuition, they are right, and for this cause; the one quality on which woman's value and influence depend, is the renunciation of self, and the old prejudices respecting her, inculcated self-renunciation. Educated in obscurity, trained to consider the fulfilment of domestic duties as the aim and end of her existence, there was little to feed the appetite for fame, or the indulgence of self-idolatry. Now, here the principle fundamentally bears upon the very qualities most desirable to be cultivated, and those most desirable to be avoided. A return to the practical part of the system is by no means to be recommended, for with increasing intellectual advantages, it is not to be supposed that the perfection of the conjugal character is to consult a husband's palate, and submit to his ill-humour,— or of the maternal, to administer in due alternation the sponge and the rod. All that is contended for is, that the fundamental principle is right—"that women were to live for others;" and, therefore, all that we have to do is to carry out this fundamentally right principle into wider application. It may easily be done if the cultivation of intellectual powers

5

be carried on with the same views and motives as
were formerly the knowledge of domestic duties,
for the benefit of immediate relations, and for the
fulfilment of appointed duties. If society at large be
benefitted by such cultivation, so much the better;
but it ought to be no part of the training of women
to consider, with any personal views, what effect
they shall produce in, or on society at large.   The
greatest benefit which they can confer upon society
is to be what they ought to be in all their domestic
relations; that is, to be what they ought to be, in
all the comprehensiveness of the term, as adapted
to the present state of society.   Let no woman
fancy that she can, by any exertion or services, compensate for the neglect of her own peculiar duties as
such.   It is by no means my intention to assert,
that women should be passive and indifferent spec-
tators of the great political questions, which affect the well-being of community, neither can I
repeat the old adage, that " women have nothing
to do with politics."   They have, and ought to have
much to do with politics.   But in what way?   It
has been maintained, that their public participation
in them would be fatal to the best interests of society.   How, then, are women to interfere in politics?
As moral agents; as representatives of the moral
principle; as champions of the right in preference
to the expedient; by their endeavours to instil into
their relatives of the other sex the uncompromising

sense of duty and self-devotion, which ought to be *their* ruling principles! The immense influence which women possess will be most beneficial, if allowed to flow in its natural channels, viz: domestic ones,—because it is of the utmost importance to the existence of influence, that purity of motive be unquestioned. It is by no means affirmed, that women's political feelings are always guided by the abstract principles of right and wrong; but they are surely more likely to be so, if they themselves are restrained from the public expression of them. Participation in scenes of popular emotion has a natural tendency to warp conscience and overcome charity. Now conscience and charity (or love) are the very essence of woman's beneficial influence, therefore everything tending to blunt the one and sour the other is seduously to be avoided by her. It is of the utmost importance to men to feel, in consulting a wife, a mother, or a sister, that they are appealing *from* their passions and prejudices, and not *to* them as embodied in a second self: nothing tends to give opinions such weight as the certainty, that the utterer of them is free from all petty or personal motives. The beneficial influence of woman is nullified if once her motives, or her personal character, come to be the subject of attack, and this fact alone ought to induce her patiently to acquiesce in the plan of seclusion from public affairs.

It supposes, indeed, some magnanimity in the possessors of great powers and widely extended influence, to be willing to exercise them with silent unostentatious vigilance. There must be a deeper principle than usually lies at the root of female education, to induce women to acquiesce in the plan, which, assigning to them the responsibility, has denied them the *éclat* of being reformers of society. Yet it is, probably, exactly in proportion to their reception of this truth, and their adoption of it into their hearts, that they will fulfil their own high and lofty mission; precisely because the manifestation of such a spirit is the one thing needful for the regeneration of society. It is from her being the depository and disseminator of such a spirit, that woman's influence is principally derived. It appears to be for this end that Providence has so lavishly endowed her with moral qualities, and, above all, with that of love,—the antagonist spirit of selfish worldliness,—that spirit which, as it is vanquished or victorious, bear with it the moral destinies of the world! Now it is proverbially as well as scripturally true, that love "seeketh not its own" interest, but the good of others, and finds its highest honour, its highest happiness, in so doing. This is precisely the spirit which can never be too much cultivated by women, because it is the spirit by which their highest tri- *umphs are to be* achieved: it is they who are called upon to show forth its beauty, and to prove its power; every thing in their education should tend to develope self-devotion and self-renunciation. How far existing systems contribute to this object it must be our next step to inquire.

5*

CHAPTER VI.

EDUCATION OF WOMEN.

And now I see, with eye serene,
The very pulse of the machine ;
A being, breathing thoughtful breath,
A traveller betwixt life and death ;
The reason fair, the temperate will,
Endurance, foresight, strength, and skill,.
A perfect woman, nobly planned,
To warn, to comfort, and command ;
And yet a Spirit still, and bright
With something of an Angel light. .

WORDSWORTH.

ON THE PRESENT STATE OF FEMALE EDUCATION ;. ITS BEARINGS ON WOMEN'S DUTIES.

["THE education of women is more important than that of men, since that of men is always their work."*]

We are now to consider how far the present systems of female education tend to the great end here mentioned, the truth of which, reflection and experience combine to prove. Great is the boast of the progress of education ; great would be the

* Aimé Martin.

indignation excited by a doubt as to the fact of this progress. ["A simple question will express this doubt more forcibly, and place this subject in a stronger light: 'Are women qualified to educate men?' If they are not, no available progress has been made. In the very heart of civilized Europe, are women what they ought to be? and does not their education prove how little we know the consequences of neglecting it?"*] Is it possible to believe, that upon their training depends the happiness of families—the well-being of nations? The selfishness, political and social; the forgetfulness of patriotism; the unregulated tempers and low ambition of the one sex, testify but too clearly how little has been done by the vaunted education of the other. For education is useless, or at least neutral, if it do not bear upon duty, as well as upon cultivation, if it do not expand the soul, while it enlightens the intellect.

How far expansion of soul, or enlightenment of intellect, is to be expected from the present systems of female education, we have seen in effects, —let us now go back to causes.

It is unnecessary to start from the prejudice of ignorance; it is now universally acknowledged, that women have a right to education, and that they must be educated. We smile with conde-

* Aimé Martin.

scending piety at the blinded state of our respected grandmothers, and thank God that we are not as they, with a thanksgiving as uncalled for as that of the proud Pharisee.   On abstract ground their education was better than ours; it was a preparation for their future duties.   It does not affect the question, that their notion of these duties was entirely confined to the physical comfort of husbands and children.   The defect of the scheme, as has been argued, was not in rationality, but in comprehensiveness,—a fundamentally right principle being the basis, it is easy to extend the application of it indefinitely.

Indiscriminate blame, however, is as invidious as it is useless; if the fault-finder be not also the fault-mender, the exercise of his powers is, at best, but a negative benefit.   Let us, therefore, enter into a calm examination of the two principal ramifications, into which education has insensibly divided itself, as far as the young women of our own country are concerned; bearing in mind that women can only exercise their true influence, inasmuch as they are free from worldly-mindedness and egotism, and that, therefore, no system of education can be good which does not tend to subdue the selfish, and bring out the unselfish principle. The systems alluded to are these :—

1st.   The education of accomplishments for *shining* in society.

2d. Intellectual education, or that of the mental powers.

What are the objects of either? To prepare the young for life; its subsequent trials; its weighty duties; its inevitable termination? We will examine the principles on which both these educations are made to work, and see whether, or how far, they have any relation to those most called for, by the future and presumed duties of the educated. The worldly and the intellectual, alternately objects of contempt to each other, are equally objects of pity to the wise, as mistaken in their end, and deceived as to the means of attaining that end.

The education of accomplishments, (especially as conducted in this country,) would be a risible, if it were not a painful subject of contemplation. Intense labour; immense sums of money; hours, nay, days of valuable time! What a list of sacrifices! Now for results. Of the many who thus sacrifice time, health, and property, how few attain even a moderate proficiency. The love of beauty, the power of self-amusement (if obtained) might, in some degree, justify these sacrifices; they are valuable ends in themselves, still more valuable from contingent advantages. There is a deep influence hidden under these beautiful arts, —an influence far deeper than the world in its thoughtlessness, or the worldly student in his vanity, ever can know,—an influence refining,

consoling, elevating : they afford a channel in
which the lofty aspirings, the unsatisfied year
ings of the pure and elevated in soul may po
themselves. The perception of the beautiful
next to the love of our fellow-creatures, the mc
purely unselfish of all our natural emotions, a
is, therefore, a most powerful engine in the han
of those who regard selfishness as the giant pa
sion, whose castle must be stormed before a
other conquest can be begun, and in vanquishi
whom all lawful and innocent weapons should, l
turns, be employed.

Let us consider how we employ this migh
ally of virtue and loftiness of soul. Into the ci
tivation of the arts, disguised under the hackney
name of accomplishments, does one particle of i
tellectuality creep? Would not many of the
ablest professors and most diligent practitione
stare, with unfeigned wonder, at the suppositic
that the five hours per diem devoted to the pia
and the easel, had any other object than to acco
plish the fingers? The idea of their influenci
the head, would be ridiculous! of their improvi
the heart, preposterous! Yet if both head a
heart do not combine in these pursuits, how c
the cultivators justify to themselves the devoti
of time and labour to their acquisition : time a
labour, in many cases, abstracted from the pe
formance of present, or preparation for futu

EDUCATION OF WOMEN. **59**

duties,—this is especially applicable to the middle classes of society.

Let us now turn to the issues of this education ! The accomplishments acquired at such cost must be displayed. To whom ? the possessor has no delight in them,—her immediate relatives, perhaps, no taste for them,—to strangers, therefore. It is not necessary to make many strictures on this subject; the rage for universal exhibition has been written and talked down : in fact, there are great hopes for the world in this particular ; it has descended so low in the scale of society, that we trust it will soon be exploded altogether. The fashion, therefore, need not be here treated of, but the spirit which it has engendered, and which will survive its parent. This, as influencing the female character—especially the maternal—bears greatly upon the point in view ;—to live for the applause of the foolish *many*, instead of the approbation of the well-judging *few;* to rule duty, conscience, morals, by a low worldly standard ; to view worldly admiration as the aim, and worldly aggrandizement as the end of life ; these are a few,—a very few,—indications of this spirit, and these have infected every rank, from the highest to the middle and lower classes of society. To every thing gentle or refined, to every thing lofty or dignified in the female character, this spirit is utterly opposed. Refinement would teach to shun the vulgar ap-

plause which almost insults its object,—dig
would shrink from displaying before hea'r
crowds those emotions of the soul, without w
all art is vulgar,—and how can women, who l
neither refinement nor dignity, retail that influ
which, rightly used, is to be so great an engii
the regeneration of society? How can the
and selfish exhibitor of paltry acquirements
mature into the mother of the Gracchi,—the
lary guardian of the rising virtues of the comi
wealth? It is in vain to hope it.

Before making any strictures on intellec
education, it is necessary to enter into a shor
planation, for it is not denied that rightly-cul
ted mental power is a great good. The kin
cultivation which is here decried, is open to
same objections as the last mentioned. It is
cultivation of power, with a view, not to the
piness of the individual, but to her fame; nc
her usefulness, but to her brilliancy. We l
only to look round society, and see that inte
has its vanity as well as beauty or accomp
ments, and that its effects are more mischiev
It has a hardening, deadening kind of influei
the more so, that the so-called mental cultiva
frequently consists only of a pedantic heaping
of information, valuable indeed in itself, but w
ing the principle of combination to make it us
Stones and bricks are valuable things, very v

able; but they are not beautiful or useful till the hand of the architect has given them a form, and the cement of the bricklayer has knit them together. It is a fine expression of Miss Edgeworth, in speaking of the mind of one of her heroines, " that the stream of literature had passed over it, was apparent only from its fertility." Intellectual cultivation was too long considered as education, properly so called. The mischief which this error has produced, is exactly in proportion to the increase of power thereby communicated to wrong principles.

What, then, is the true object of female education ? The best answer to this question is, a statement of future duties; for it must never be forgotten, that if education be not a training for future duties, it is nothing. The ordinary lot of woman is to marry. Has any thing in these educations prepared her to make a wise choice in marriage? To be a mother ! Have the duties of maternity,— the nature of moral influence,—been pointed out to her ? Has she ever been enlightened as to the consequent unspeakable importance of personal character as the source of influence ? In a word, have any means, direct or indirect, prepared her for her duties? No! but she is a linguist, a pianist, graceful, admired. What is that to the purpose? The grand evil of such an education, is the mistaking means for ends; a common error, and the source of half the moral confusion exist-

ing in the world.   It is the substitution of the part
for a whole.   The time when young women enter
upon life, is the one point to which all plans of
education tend, and at which they all terminate :
and to prepare them for that point, is the object of
their training.   Is it not cruel to lay up for them
a store of future wretchedness, by an education
which has no period in view but one ; a very short
one, and the most unimportant and irresponsible
of the whole of life ?   Who that had the power of
choice would choose to buy the admiration of the
world for a few short years with the happiness of
a whole life ? the temporary power to dazzle and
to charm, with the growing sense of duties undertaken only to be neglected, and responsibilities,
the existence of which is discovered perhaps si-
multaneously with that of an utter inability to
meet them ?   Even if the mischief stopped here,
it would be sufficiently great ; but the craving ap_
petite for applause once roused, is not so easily
lulled again.   The moral energies, pampered by
unwholesome nourishment,—like the body when
disordered by luxurious dainties,—refuse to perform their healthy functions, and thus is occasioned a perpetual strife and warfare of internal
principles ; the selfish principle still seeking the
accustomed gratification, the conjugal and maternal prompting to the performance of duty.   But
duty is a cold word ; and people, in order to find

pleasure in duty, must have been trained to con-
·sider their duties as pleasures. This is a truth at
which no one arrives by inspiration! And in this
moral struggle, which, like all other struggles, produces lassitude and distaste of all things, the happiness of the individual is lost, her usefulness destroyed, her influence most pernicious. For nothing has so injurious an effect on temper and
manners, and consequently on moral influence, as
the want of that internal quiet which can only
arise from the accordance of duty with inclination.
Another most pernicious effect is, the deadening
within the heart of the feeling of love, which is the
root of all influence; for it is an extraordinary fact,
that vanity acts as a sort of refrigerator on all men,
on the possessor of it, and on the observer.

Now, if conscientiousness and unselfishness be
the two main supports of women's beneficial influence, how can any education be good which has
not the cultivation of these qualities for its first and
principal object? The grand objects, then, in the
education of women ought to be, the conscience,
the heart, and the affections; the developement
of those moral qualities which Providence has so
liberally bestowed upon them, doubtless with a
wise and beneficent purpose. Originators of conscientiousness, how can they implant what they
have never cultivated, nor brought to maturity in
themselves? Sovereigns of the affections, how

can they direct the kingdom whose laws they have not studied, the springs of whose government are concealed from them? The conscience and the affections being primarily enlightened, all other cultivation, as secondary, is most valuable. Intelligence, accomplishments, even external elegance, become objects of importance, as assisting the influence which women have, and exert too often for unworthy ends, but which in this case could not fail to be beneficial. Let the light of intellect, and the charm of accomplishments, be the willing handmaids of cultivated and enlightened conscience. Cultivate the intellect with reference to the conscience, that views of duty may be comprehensive, as well as just; cultivate the imagination still with reference to the conscience, that those inward aspirations, which all indulge, more or less, may be turned from the gauds of an idle and vain imagination, and shed over daily life and daily duty the halo of a poetic influence; cultivate the manners, that the qualities of heart and head may have an additional auxiliary in obtaining that influence by which a mighty regeneration is to be worked. The issues of such an education will justify the claims made for women in these pages; then the spirit of vanity will yield to the spirit of self-devotion: that spirit confessedly natural to women, and only perverted by wrong education. *Content* with the sphere of usefulness assigned her

by Nature and Nature's God, viewing that sphere
with the piercing eye of intellect, and gilding it
with the beautiful colours of the imagination, she
will cease the vain and almost impious attempt to
wander from it. She will see and acknowledge
the beauty, the harmony of the arrangement which
has made her physical inferiority (the only inferiority which we acknowledge) the very root from
which spring her virtues and their attendant influences. Removed from the actual collision of
political contests, and screened from the passions
which such engender, she brings party questions
to the test of the unalterable principles of reason
and religion; she is, so to speak, the guardian angel of man's political integrity, liable at the best to
be warped by passion or prejudice, and excited by
the rude clashing of opinions and interests. This
is the true secret of woman's political influence,
the true object of her political enlightenment. Governments will never be perfect till all distinction
between private and public virtue, private and
public honour, be done away! Who so fit an
agent for the operation of this change as enlightened, unselfish woman? Who so fit, in her two-
fold capacity of companion and early instructor,
to teach men to prefer honour to gain, duty to ease,
public to private interests, and God's work to
man's inventions? And shall it be said that women have no political existence, no political influ-

ence, when the very germs of political regeneration
may spring from them alone, when the fate of nations yet unborn may depend upon the use which
they make of the mighty influences committed to
their care? The blindness which sees not how
these influences would be lessened by taking her
out of the sphere assigned by Providence, if voluntary, is wicked—if real, is pitiable. As well might
we desire the earth's beautiful satellite to give
place to a second sun, thereby producing the in-
tolerable and glaring continuity of perpetual day.
Those who would be the agents of Providence,
must observe the workings of Providence, and be
content to work also in that way, and by those
means, which Almighty wisdom appoints. There
is infinite littleness in despising small things. It
seems paradoxical to say that there are no small
things; our littleness and our aspiration make
things appear small. There are, morally speaking,
no small duties. Nothing that influences human
virtue and happiness can be really trifling,—and
what more influences them than the despised, because limited, duties assigned to woman? It is
true, her reward (her task being done) is not of
this world, nor will she wish it to be—enough for
her to be one of the most active and efficient agents
in her heavenly Father's work of man's regeneration,—enough for her that generations yet unborn
shall rise up and call her blessed.

CHAPTER VII.

EDUCATION, CONTINUED.—LOVE—MARRIAGE.

It is a golden chain let down from heaven
Whose links are bright and even,
That falls like sleep on lovers, and combines
The soft and sweetest minds
In equal knots ; this bears no brands, nor darts,
But in a calm and godlike unity
Preserves community.
Richer than time, and as time's value rare,
Sober as saddest care.

BEN JONSON.

Marriage is matter of more worth
Than to be dealt in by attorneyship.

SHAKSPEARE.

'HE conventual and monastic origin of all systems of education has had a very injurious influence, on that of women especially, because the
conventual spirit has been longer retained in it.

If no education be good which does not bear
upon the future duties of the educated, it follows
that the systematic exclusion of any one subject
connected with, or bearing upon, future duties,
must be an evil. The wisdom of employing those
who had renounced the world to form the minds of
those who were to mix in it, to be exposed in all its

allurements, to share in all its duties, was doub
ful indeed; and the danger was enhanced by th
fact, that the majority of recluses were anythir
but indifferent to the world which they had r
nounced. The convent was too often the refug
of disappointed worldliness, the grave of blaste
hopes, or the prison of involuntary victims;
withering atmosphere this in which to place war
young hearts, and expect them to expand ar
flourish. The evil effects would be varied accor
ing to the different characters submitted to its i
fluence. The sensitive entered upon life oppresse
with fears and terrors; with a conscience morbi
not enlightened; bewildered by the impossibility
reconciling principles and duties. The ardent ar
sanguine, longing to escape from restraint, picture
to themselves in these unknown and untried r
gions, delights infinite and unvaried; and seeir
the incompatibility of inculcated principles ar
worldly pleasures, discarded principle altogethe
It is needless to pursue this subject further, becau
a universal assent will (in this country, at leas
await the remarks here made; their applicabili
to what follows may not at first be so apparer
The conventual spirit has survived conventual i
stitutions,—in the department of female educatic
especially.

In the first place, the instructors of female you
are considered respectable and trustworthy only

proportion as they cease to be young, or at least in proportion as they appear to forget that they ever were so. Any touch of sympathy for the follies of childhood, or the indiscretions of youth, would blast the prospects of a candidate for that honourable office, and, in the opinion of many, render her unfit for its fulfilment. The unfitness is attached to the opposite disposition ; for the very fact of its existence is as effectual an obstacle to her being a good trainer of youth, as if she had taken a vow never to see the world but through an iron grating. Experience can never benefit youth, except when combined with indulgence. The instructor who, from the heights of past temptations and subdued passion, looks down with cool watchfulness on the struggles of his youthful pupil, will see him lie floundering in the mire, or perishing in the deep water. He must retrace his own steps, take him by the hand, and sustain him, till he is passed the dangerous and slippery paths of youth. He must become as a little child to the young and frail being committed to his care, and whose welfare and safety depend (in great measure) upon him. A cold and unloving admiration never will produce imitation: it is like the hopeless love of poor Helena :—

'Twere all as one, as I should love a bright particular star !

Here, then, the conventual spirit has been in injurious *operation ;*—no less so on other points.

This conventual prejudice has banished 1
our school-rooms the name of love, and
sented to their youthful inmates fragments
stead of books, cramped and puny publicat
instead, of the works of master-spirits, lest
mind should be contaminated by any allu
to that passion contained in them.   The wis
of such a proceeding is much upon a par
that which devoted the feet to stocks and
shoulders to backboards, in order to make t
elegant, and denied them heaven's air and ac
exercise through care for their health.   The re
in the one case as in the other, is disease and
tortion.   Nature will assert her rights over
beings she has made ; and she avenges, by
production of deformity, all attempts to forc
shackle her operations.   The golden globe c
not check the expansive force of water ; equ
useless is it to attempt any check on the expan
force of mind,—it will ooze out !   We ought
ago to have been convinced, that the only po
allowed to us is the power of direction.   If
half the amount of effort expanded to useless
deavours to cramp and check, has been tur
towards this channel, how different would be
results !   It is true that it is easier to check 1
to guide,—to fetter than to restrain ; and tha
attempt to remove evil by the first-occurring re
dy is a natural impulse.   But a pause sh

be made, lest in applying the remedy a worse evil be not engendered. Distorted spines and " pale consumptions," the result of the one mistake, are trifling evils, when compared with the moral evils resulting from the other. For if, as is affirmed, no education can be good which does not bear upon future duties, how can that be wise which keeps love and its temptations, maternity and its responsibilities, out of view? Who would believe that this love, so denounced, so guarded against, so carefully banished from the minds of young women, is the one principle on which their future happiness may be founded or wrecked? It is sure to seek them, (most of them, at least,) like death in the fable, to find them unprepared,—too often to leave them wretched.

Meanwhile, these exaggerated precautions in the education of one sex, have been met by equally fatal negligence in the education of the other ; and while to girls have been denied the very thoughts of love,—even in its noblest and purest form,—the most effeminate and corrupt productions of the heathen writers have been unhesitatingly laid open to boys; so that the two sexes, on whose respective notions of this passion depends the ennobling or the degrading of their race, meet on these terms : —the men know nothing of love but what they have imbibed from an impure and polluted source; the *women, nothing* at all, or nothing but what

they have clandestinely gathered from so
almost equally corrupt.   The deterioration o
feeling must follow from such injudicious trai
more especially a feeling so susceptible as lo
assuming such differing aspects.

Let no sober-minded person be startled a
deductions hence drawn, that it is foolish to b
all thoughts of love from the minds of the yo
since it is certain that girls will think, though
may not read or speak, of love ; and that no
care can preserve them from being exposed
later period, to its temptations, might it not be
to use here the directing, not the repressing,
er ?   Since women will love, might it not
well to teach them to love wisely ?   Where
wisdom of letting the combatant go unarme(
the field, in order to spare him the prospec
combat ?   Are not women made to love, a
be loved : and does not their future destin
often depend upon this passion ?   And ye
conventual prejudice which banishes its
subsists still.

[" Mothers forget, in presence of their chi
all the dangers with which this prejudice ha
rounded themselves ; the illusions which
from that ignorance, and the weakness
springs from those illusions.   To open the
of the young to the nature of true love, is t
them against the frivolous passions which

its name, for in exalting the faculties of the soul, we annihilate, in a great degree, the delusion of the senses."*]

Examine the first choice of a young girl. Of all the qualities which please her in a lover, there is, perhaps, not one which is valuable in a husband. Is not this the most complete condemnation of all our systems of education? From the fear of too much agitating the heart, we hide from women all that is worthy of love, all the depth and dignity of that passion when felt for a worthy object ;—their eye is captivated, the exterior pleases, the heart and mind are not known, and after six months union, they are surprised to find the beau ideal metamorphosed into a fool or a coxcomb. This is the issue of what are ordinarily called love-matches, because they are considered as such. "Cupid is indeed often blamed for deeds in which he has no share." In the opinion of the wise, the mischief is occasioned by the action of vivid imaginations upon minds unprepared by previous reflection on the subject; that is, by the entire banishment of all thoughts of love from education. We should endeavour, then, to engrave on the soul a model of virtue and excellence, and teach young women to regulate their affections by an approximation to this model ; the result would not be an increased

* Aimé Martin.

facility in giving the affections, but a greater difficulty in so doing; for women, whose blindness
and ignorance now make them the victims of fancied perfections, would be able to make a clear-
sighted appreciation of all that is excellent, and
have an invincible repugnance to an union not
founded upon that basis. Love, in the common
acceptation of the term, is a folly,—love, in its
purity, its loftiness, its unselfishness, is not only a
consequence, but a proof of our moral excellence,—
the sensibility to moral beauty, the forgetfulness of
self in the admiration engendered by it, all prove
its claim to be a high moral influence; it is the
triumph of the unselfish over the selfish part of
our nature.*

What is meant by educating young women to
love wisely is simply this, that they be taught to
distinguish true love from the false spirit which
usurps its name and garb; that they be taught to
abstract from it the worldliness, vanity, and folly,
with which it has been mixed up. They should
be taught that it is not to be the amusement of an
idle hour; the indulgence of a capricious and gree-
dy vanity; the ladder, by the assistance of which
they may climb a few steps higher in the grades of
society; in short, that except it owe its origin to

[* It is Coleridge who speaks of the "unselfishness of love,"
in one of the volumes of his "Remains."]

the noble qualities of heart and mind, it is nothing but a contemptible weakness, to be pitied perhaps, but not to be indulged or admired.

When the mighty influence of this passion is considered, the important relations and weighty responsibilities to which it gives rise, we have reason to be astonished at the levity with which the subject is treated by the world at large, and the unconsciousness and indifference with which those responsibilities are assumed. It is like the madman who flings about firebrands and calls it sport. The remedy for this evil must begin with the sex who have in their hands that powerful influence, the liberty of rejection. Let them not complain that liberty of choice is not theirs; it would only increase their responsibilities without adding to their happiness or to their usefulness. The liberty which they do possess is amply sufficient to ensure for them the power of being benefactors of mankind. As soon as the noble and elevated of our sex shall refuse to unite on any but moral and intellectual grounds with the other, so soon will a mighty regeneration begin to be effected: and this end will, perhaps, be better served by the simple liberty of rejection than by liberty of choice. Rejection is never inflicted without pain; it is never received without humiliation, however unfounded, (for simply to want the power of pleasing can be no disgrace); but in the existence of this conven-

tional feeling we find the source of a deep influence.   If women would, as by one common league
and covenant, agree to use this powerful engine in
defence of morals, what a change might they not
effect in the tone of society !   Is it not a subject
that ought to crimson every woman's cheek with
shame, that the want of moral qualifications is
generally the very last cause of rejection ?   If the
worldly find the wealth, and the intellectual the
intelligence, which they seek in a companion,
there are few who will not shut their eyes in wil-
ful and convenient blindness to the want of such
qualifications.   It is a fatal error which has bound
up the cause of affection so intimately with worldly considerations; and it is a growing evil.   The
increasing demands of luxury in a highly civilized
community operate most injuriously on the cause
of disinterested affections, and particularly so in
the case of women, who are generally precluded
from maintaining or advancing their place in society by any other schemes than matrimonial ones.
I might say something here on the cruelty of that
conventional prejudice which shackles the inde-
pendence of women, by attaching the loss of caste
to almost all, nay, all, of the very few sources of
pecuniary emolument open to them.   It requires
great strength of principle to disregard this prejudice ; and while urged by duty to inveigh against
mercenary unions, I feel some compunction at the

thoughts of the numerous class who are in a manner forced by this prejudice into forming them. But there are too many who have no such excuse, and to them the remaining observations are addressed. The sacred nature of the conjugal relation is entirely merged in the worldly aspect of it. That union sacred, indissoluble, fraught with all that earth has to bestow of happiness or misery, is entered upon much on the plan and principle of a partnership account in mercantile affairs—each bringing his or her quantum of worldly possessions —and often with even less inquiry as to moral qualities, than persons so situated would make ; God's ordinances are not to be so mocked, and such violations of his laws are severely visited upon offenders against them. It would be laughable, if it were not too melancholy, to see beings bound by the holiest ties, who ought to be the sharers in the most sacred duties—united, perhaps, but in one aim, and *that* to secure from a world which cares not for them, a few atoms more of external observance and attention: to this noble aim sacrificing their own ease and comfort, and the future prospects of those dependent on them. If half the sacrifice thus made to the imperious demands of fashion, (and which is received with the indifference it deserves,) were exerted in a good cause, what benefits might it not produce ?

While women are thus content to sacrifice deli-

7*

cacy, affection, principle, to the desire of worldly
establishment or aggrandizement, how is the regeneration of society to be expected from them?
Formerly, too, this spirit was confined to the old,
hackneyed in the ways of the world, and who,
having worn out the trifling affections which they
ever had, would subject those of their children to
the maxims of worldly prudence. This we learn
from fiction and the drama, where the worldly
wisdom of age is always represented as opposed
to the generous but imprudent passions of youth.
But now, in these our better and more enlightened
days, those mercenary maxims which were odious
even in age, are found in the mouths of the young
and the fair,—or at least, if not in their mouths, in
their actions. To sacrifice affection to interest is
a praiseworthy thing. It is fearful to hear the
withering sneer with which that folly, love, is
spoken of by young and innocent lips—a sneer of
conscious superiority too! It is a superiority not
to be envied, and which makes them objects of
greater pity than those whom they affect to despise.
There is no subject so sacred that it has not a side
open to ridicule, and all the most pure and noble
attributes of our nature may be converted into
subjects for a jest, by minds in which no lofty idea
can find an echo. All notions of unworldly and
unselfish attachment are branded with the name
of romantic follies, unworthy of sensible persons;

and the idealities of love, like all other idealities, are fast disappearing beneath the leaden mantle of expediency.

The reform must begin here, as in all great moral questions, with the arbiters of morals—those from whom morals take their tone—women. That we have no right to expect it to begin with the other sex, may be proved even by a vulgar aphorism. It is often triumphantly said, that "a man may marry when he will—a woman must marry when she can." How keen a satire upon both sexes is couched in this homely proverb! and how long will they consent not only patiently to acquiesce in its truth, but to prove it by their actions? That women may be able thus to reform society, it is of importance that conscience be educated on this subject as on every other: educated, too, before the tinsel of false romance deceive the eye, or the frost of worldly-mindedness congeal the heart of youth. It seems to me that this object would best be effected, not by avoiding the subject of love, but by treating it, when it arises, with seriousness and simplicity, as a feeling which the young may one day be called upon to excite and to return, but which can have no existence in the lofty in soul and pure in heart, except when called forth by corresponding qualities in another. Such training as this would be a far more effectual preventive of foolish passions, than cramping the

intellect in narrow ignorance, and excluding all
knowledge of what life is—in order to prepare
people for entering upon it : a plan about as wise
in itself, and as successful as to results, as the bolts,
bars, and duennas of a Spanish play. Outward,
substituted for inward restraints, are sure to act
upon man mentally, as actual bonds do physical-
ly ; he only wants to get free from them.   Noble
and virtuous principles in the heart, will not fail
to direct the conduct aright, and it is to transfer
these things from matters of decorum or expediency, to matters of conscience, that we should use
our most earnest endeavours.   Above all, it is in-
cumbent upon those who have the training of the
young—of women especially—so to imbue their
souls with lofty and conscientious principles of
action, that they may be alike unwilling to deceive, or liable to be deceived ; that they may not
be led as fools or as victims into those responsible
relations, for the consequences of which, (how
momentous !) to themselves, to others, and to society at large, they are answerable to a God of
infinite wisdom and justice.

CHAPTER VIII.

MATERNAL LOVE.

A mother goes out of herself to live in her child.
                                                    LINDSAY.

{"ALL our earthly attachments are inspired by pleasure: maternal love, alone, takes its rise in the midst of suffering. This power, superior to suffering itself, is, however, only an animal sensation—a blind instinct which belongs to the insect, to the quadruped, to the bird, as to the woman: an immutable law of Nature—nothing more.

"In beings inferior to man we see the operation of this instinct, associating itself with the passions, doubling their power, and raising them almost to intelligence. The bird forms its nest before it knows that it is about to produce anything of which it must take care: it lines that nest with a delicate down before it knows the delicacy of its brood: it sits, that is to say, the most restless of beings sits, immoveable during several weeks upon a lifeless egg, before it knows that it encloses a being like itself. At length, the young ones being hatched, it brings their food, it drives away their enemies,

is anxious for their preservation; and all these la-
bours, painful or pleasurable, are to remain without a recompense; no filial tenderness will ever
respond to this maternal tenderness. One day, the
little ones try their wings—another, they take their
flight and wing their way into the plains of air.
The animals have no family—they have none of
the true parental affection—they are the servants
of Nature.

"A fact worthy of remark is, that maternal love
only lasts in each animal the time necessary for
the preservation of the species: as soon as the little
ones have ceased to need their mother, their mother abandons them. In the morning the mother
would have waged the most furious warfare for her
young ones, whom in the evening she cannot re-
cognise. And this indifference awakens no regret,
leaves no remembrance, enters the mind at the very
time when gratitude, and habits, long formed, seem
to render it impossible. When we reflect that the
order and harmony of the world are maintained by
this double law of love and indifference, we are
astonished that it does not excite more attention.
Let us only imagine what a new order of things
the durable affection of animals would introduce
upon this globe, what a power added to their exter-
minating instincts! Let the war-cry be heard, and
twenty generations rally round one female—whole
families will be armed, and all these armies will

work in the labour of destruction. To prevent
this destruction, to establish the balance between
life and death, the law of indifference suffices.
There is one exception, and only one—this exception is found in the heart of the woman—there
alone is maternal love, a durable sentiment, because it is a moral one."*]

The true maternal love—the human—begins
where the animal terminates. It is a startling fact,
that maternal love, the theme of poetry, and the
type of every other pure affection, is, in its origin,
only the most beautiful of instincts. Nor is it till
we see the union of this instinct with a moral affection that we have maternal love, in its dignity
and regenerating power. The fondness of some
mothers for their children is simply the selfish
gratification of an animal passion, regardless of
anything but its own present enjoyment, and su-
premely regardless of the ultimate happiness of
its object. It is the transferred idolatry of a selfish
nature to a second self. This is not the maternal
love which we must call to our aid as a regenerating principle—certainly, it is not fit to speak
slightingly of the love and care bestowed on infancy; ["but women ought to know,—and how shall
they know if no one dare to tell them ?—that they
are only *mothers* in the true sense and compre-

* Aimé Martin.

hensive dignity of the term, if they labour in developing the souls of her children. Their mission on earth is not to bring forth an intelligent biped—it is a man which the world demands from them, a man whose soul is penetrated with virtue—who knows how to choose his companion, inspire virtue into his children, and, if needful, to lay down his life at the shrine of duty. Woman, then, has a two-fold duty, as man has a two-fold birth. To be born into the world is only to be born to pain or pleasure: to be born to the love of God and man, is the true existence, and this second birth our mother owes us, if she wishes for a higher happiness than that of watching us while we breathe and digest. This is the happiness which Shakspeare expresses so well when he makes the mother of Coriolanus say, that she felt more pleasure in hearing that he had performed an honourable action, than in the first joys of maternity."*]

Let us see how the different kinds of love are exemplified. The natural instinct, and the moral principle. The natural instinct will prompt the weakest and most criminal of women to confront pain, danger, death itself, for her offspring, but it will not enable a mother, unaided by other principles, to correct one failing, to subdue one passion, to avoid one selfish or criminal indulgence, for its sake.

Aimé Martin.

The instinct induces a mother to bestow fondness and caresses on her child, to tend its sick couch, to watch over its health and comfort, regardless of her own. Beautiful manifestations of a beautiful and kind provision of Providence! But except that mother have the courage to deny her child's unreasonable desires, to thwart it, (even on the bed of sickness and in the hour of glee,) if its future moral interests require it, we must confine our admirations to the instinct, and withhold it from the individual.* This is the true maternal affection, the true developement of that divine and holy love to man, which, regardless of inferior considerations, seeks only his moral and ultimate good. If what has been said be true, it is proved that the maternal feeling, shared by woman with the lower animals, can lay no claim to the character of a moral influence—that, however beautiful and worthy of admiration the manifestations of it may be, they possess no power of calling forth answering manifestations in their object. Nay, after it has prompted and performed the physical cares called forth by the helplessness of infancy, it *may have*, and often has, an influence positively pernicious. This may serve to account for a fact so well known as to be proverbial—but of which, as far as I know, no philosophical explanation has

[* This is worthy of the highest consideration.]

8

yet been attempted, viz: that spoiled childrer
always selfish; in other words, they receivec
expression of passionate affection unconscic
and ungratefully, and give no affection in re
Now it is to be remarked that the effects prod:
by any influence, respond exactly in *their* n&
to the nature of that influence. And this
account for the fact, that the passionate indulg
of instinctive fondness, unrestrained by moral
ciple in any of its manifestations, produces—nc
swering fondness—but coldness and indiffer&
Here the nature of the effects responds to the n&
of the influence. The influence is an exhit
of selfishness—the effect is an exhibition of se
ness likewise—unthankfulness and insubor&
tion. On the contrary, the exhibition of the n
principle is unselfish, for I suppose that none
a mother can know the self-sacrifice requisit&
the exercise of it in repressing the instinct.
effect responds—it is the production of unse
ness likewise—obedience and gratitude.

Enough has been said on this subject to re
some errors, which women especially are liat
fall into, respecting the value and efficacy of m
nal instinct. These errors are by no means ι
tural ones, for so beautiful are the various f·
under which it appears, that admiration natu
enough induces forgetfulness of moral c&
quences. Yet it is of the utmost importance

these errors be rectified, for they have a wide and deep influence on the well-being of mankind. An attentive observation of facts, and of the state of society, will best display their pernicious effects.

This instinctive tenderness is common to all women who are mothers; and we evidently see that it is finite in its aim and scope, by its complete sufficiency for its object, and for nothing more. *Here is the first capital error;* the disposition to trust to its accomplishing more than it was designed to accomplish,—more, in fact, than it *can* accomplish. Its proper sphere of action is the physical preservation, not the moral developement, of its object; and to presume that it is capable of procuring moral developement, or of superintending its progress, is to force it upon a task to which it is unequal. Instinctive is no more able to perform the functions of moral maternity, than abstract philosophy would be to supply to an infant the want of the necessary attentions dictated by instinctive tenderness. It is true that, as an auxiliary, it is admirable; and that the moral principle, aided by it, will be divested in its exercise of all appearance of rigour and severity, and win, instead of forcing, the young and ductile mind to obedience and virtue.

Another popular, and by no means astonishing, error, exists respecting the meritorious nature of this maternal instinct: and this error has likewise occasioned much evil. Inasmuch as it is a passion, it has no merit; and can only have merit when, by an union with the moral sense, it has become a virtue! It is not with any view of depreciating so beautiful an instinct that the distinction is made,—far from it! It will presently be seen how deeply I venerate it, and with what consummate wisdom I think it has been planted for a high purpose in woman's heart; but it is most important that women be recalled from the erroneous notions which they have formed of its nature and office, and their own consequent responsibilities. Nothing can be more distressing to a conscientious mind, than to hear the praise sometimes accorded to its blind and infatuated exercise,—except the evident self-gratulation which such applause excites. It is no uncommon thing to hear mothers lamenting the weakness which incapacitates them from exercising moral restraint over their children. Now here it is only necessary to appeal to common sense; we never publish, or publicly lament, weaknesses of which we are *really* ashamed. No. We may therefore be sure that selfishness and vanity have appropriated to themselves this passion as they would any other, as a medium of exhibition. A mother can never be sure that she is possessed of the spirit of moral maternity, except she be as willing to make moral sacrifices to her children as *physical*; to give up the cherished indulgence of

faults and follies as cheerfully as Nature prompts
. her to give up bodily ease and comfort for its sake:
in a word, except her regard for its ultimate moral
destiny transcend, by far, her anxiety for its physical well-being. These are the tests by which
mothers must be content to have their claims
tried, and by which, if they are wise, they will
try themselves. If the test fail on application,
let them be sure they are amongst those who have
undertaken most weighty responsibilities without
due preparation; who have sat down to build a
tower, without counting the cost; happy, if
strength of mind and moral power be still left to
rectify this lamentable mistake, and to repair to
themselves and to society the evils which they
have thus occasioned!

It is not then from instinctive maternal love,
but from moral maternity, that we gain the un-
bounded influence which has before been treated
of. Its existence has been proved by reasoning
and by historical facts; but that it may perform its
mission, mothers must be aware of its existence,
and of their own consequent responsibilities.
This influence consists not in the power of dog-
matizing and instructing: its main agents are two,
self-denial and example. Both pre-suppose the
existence of the spirit of self-devotion, that spirit
which I have shown it to be the particular province of female education to cultivate and direct.

8*

It demands sacrifices; but sacrifices which the instinct would never prompt, and which even love itself will not always make easy. It demands, in short, the spirit of self-renunciation, not only in the physical, but in the moral nature of the mother: and no woman ought to undertake such responsible duties without having counted the cost, and fairly estimated the probability of being able to fulfil them.

CHAPTER IX.

THE NATURE OF INFLUENCE—ITS SOURCE.

Inclines our action, not constrains our will.
POPE.

Those thousand decencies that daily flow
From all her words and actions, mixed with love.
MILTON.

IT is difficult to explain abstract conceptions in words, and to account for results of which the sources are evanescent and almost imperceptible; yet it is important to try, at least, to do so, for in all questions, especially in moral questions, it is most desirable to avoid confusion of terms. Much stress has been laid in these pages on the doctrine of influence; and the subject of influences in education is now attracting much general attention: it may therefore be worth while to settle with precision what it means. The word *influence* is one of which the original etymology has been forgotten in the current meaning annexed to it; and yet it is to the etymology that we must look, if we would gain a true notion of the thing which it represents. The secret agency, and imperceptible operation of the principle, are much more fully comprehended

by recurring to the original derivation of the word.
And it is of importance that they be comprehended,
because we are then better able to understand that
indirect influences are much more powerful than
direct ones, and why they are so,—viz: because
they act by a sort of moral contagion, and are imbibed by the receiver as they flow from their source,
without consciousness on either side. We are fortunately able to exemplify this truth by a practical
example, which is found in that inexplicable thing
called family likeness ; whereby persons of different features, complexions, and statures, resemble
each other, and also one common model, in a manner totally incomprehensible. Now it is a remarkable fact, that this common model is generally the
mother. To which of the parents soever the children may bear personal or characteristic resemblance, this family resemblance is almost sure to be
derived from the mother. The intonation of voice,
the walk, the gesture, all those nameless nothings
which constitute the resemblance, are the mother's ;
and with so few exceptions, that it may be assumed
as a law of Nature. Why the mother's personal
habits should exercise such a predominating influence over her children, it will be the object of future inquiry to learn. In the mean time, I proceed
to draw a deduction quite warranted by the facts,
that the influence of a mother's personal character
is quite as great as that of her personal qualities,

and infinitely more important, since on it depends the moral atmosphere which is to surround her children, which has been spoken of at length. We may not be able to trace the effects of the one so clearly as those of the other; for the propensity to moral imitation, though as great, is not so unchecked by counteracting influences as the propensity to physical imitation. It does not commence at so early a period, and therefore is seldom allowed so exclusive an operation. Yet even a family resemblance may be perceived, mostly derived from the character of the mother; which, whether noble or mean, true or sophisticated, gentle or ungentle, usually stamps these broad characteristic distinctions on the characters of her offspring. I proceed then,—1st. To treat of the influence of personal character. 2d. To inquire whether any qualities be more important than others in securing this influence. 3d. The bearing of these upon woman's peculiar duties.

CHAPTER X.

THE INFLUENCE OF PERSONAL CHARACTER.

There is a kind of character in thy life,
That to the observer doth thy history
Fully unfold.——
                              SHAKSPEARE.

THE immense importance of personal character is a subject, which does not enough draw the attention of individuals or society, yet it is to the power of gaining influence, what the root is to the tree,—the soul to the body.   It is doubtful if any of us can be acquainted with the infinitely minute ramifications into which this all-pervading influence extends.   A slight survey of society will enable us, in some degree, to judge of it.   There are individuals who, by the sole force of personal character, seem to render wiser, better, more elevated, all with whom they come into contact. Others, again, stand in the midst of the society in which they are placed, a moral Upas, poisoning the atmosphere around them, so that no virtue can come within their shadow and live. Family virtues descend with family estates, and hereditary vices are hardly *compensated* for by hereditary possessions.   The characters of the junior members of a family are often only reflections or modifications of those of the elder. Families retain for generations peculiarities of temper and character. The Catos were all stern, upright, inflexible ; the Guises proud and haughty at heart, though irresistibly popular and fascinating in manner. We *see* the influence which men, exalted and powerful, exert on their age, and on society ; it is difficult to believe, that a similar influence is exerted by every individual man and woman, however limited his or her sphere of life : the force of the torrent is easily calculated,—that of the under-current is hidden, yet its existence and power are no less actual.

This truth opens to the conscientious a field of duty not enough cultivated. The improvement of individual character has been too much regarded as a matter of personal concern, a duty to ourselves, —to our immediate relations perhaps, but to no others,—a matter affecting our individual happiness here, and our individual safety hereafter ! This is taking a very narrow view of a very extended subject. The work of individual self-formation is a duty, not only to ourselves and our families, but to our fellow creatures at large ; it is the best and most certainly beneficial exercise of philanthropy. It is not, it is true, very flattering to self-love to be told, that instead of mending the world, (the mania of the present day,) the best service

which we can do that world is to mend oùrse
" If each mends one, all will be mended," say
old English adage, with the deep wisdom of
popular sayings,—a wisdom amply corrobo
by the unsettled principles and defective pra
of too many of the self-elected reformers of so

It is peculiarly desirable, at this particular
ture of time, that this subject be insisted
Man, naturally a social and gregarious anime
comes every day more so. The vast undertal
the mighty movements of the present day, v
can only be carried into operation by the
bined energy of many wills, tend to destroy
viduality of thought and action, and the cons
ness of individual responsibility. The drar
complains of this fact, as it affects his art, tl
presentation of surface,—the moralist has gi
cause to complain of it, as affecting the founc
of character. If it be true, that we must not f
a multitude to do evil, it is equally true, th:
must not follow a multitude even to do goo
involve the neglect of our own peculiar d
Our first, most peremptory, and most urgent
is, the improvement of our own character ; s
public beneficence may not be neutralized b
vate selfishness,—public energy by private re
ness,—that the applause of the world may r
bought at the expense of private and dor
wretchedness. So frequent and so lamentab

the proofs of human weakness in this respect, that we are sometimes tempted to believe the opinion of the cold and sneering sceptic,* that the two ruling passions of men are the love of pleasure, and the love of action; and that all their seemingly good deeds proceed from these principles. It is not so: it is a libel on human nature: men,—even erring men,—have better motives, and higher aims; but they mistake the nature of their duties and invert their order; what should be "first is last, and the last first."

It may be wisely urged, that if men waited for the perfecting of individual character, before they joined their fellow men in those great undertakings which are to ensure benefit to the race, nothing would ever be accomplished, and society would languish in a state of passive inertness. It is far from necessarily following, that attention to private should interfere with attention to public interests; and public interests are more advanced or retarded than it is possible to believe, by the personal characters of their agitators. It is difficult to get the worldly and the selfish to see this, but it is, nevertheless, true; and there is no wisdom, political or moral, in the phrase, "Measures, not men." Measures, wise and just in themselves, are received with distrust and suspicion, because the characters of their originators are liable to distrust and suspi-

* Gibbon.

cion. Lord Chesterfield, that great master of de-
ception, was forced to pay truth the compliment
of declaring, that " the most successful diplomatist
would be a man perfectly honest and upright, who
should, at all times, and in all circumstances, say
the truth, the whole truth, and nothing but the
truth."   So the rulers of nations ought to be perfectly honest and upright ; not because such men
would be free from all error, but because the faith
of the governed in their honour would obviate the
consequences of many errors.   It is the want of
unselfishness and truth on the part of rulers, and
the consequent want of faith in the ruled, that has
reduced the politics of nations to a complicated
science.   If we could once get men to act out the
Gospel precept, " Do unto others as ye would that
they should do unto you," nations might burn their
codes, and lawyers their statute-books. These are
the hundred cords with which the Lilliputians
bound Gulliver, and he escaped.   If they had possessed it, or could have managed it, one cable
would have been worth them all. Much has been
said,—much written,—on the art of governing.
Why has the simple truth been overlooked or sup-
pressed, that the moral character of the rulers of
nations is of first-rate importance ?   Except the
Lord build the city, vain is the labour of them who
build it ; except religion and virtue guide the State,
vain are the talents and the acts of legislators. Is

it possible that motives of paltry, personal advancement, or of pecuniary gain, can induce men to assume responsibilities affecting the welfare of millions? The voice of those millions replies in the affirmative, and their reproachful glances turn on *you*, mothers of our legislators! It might have been yours, to stamp on their infant minds the dispassionate and unselfish devotedness which belongs to your own sex,—the scorn of meanness; the contempt of self, in comparison with others, peculiar to woman. How have you fulfilled your lofty mission? Charity itself can only allow us to suppose that its existence is as unknown as its spirit.

The important fact, then, of the great influence of personal character, can never be too much impressed upon all; but it is peculiarly needful that women be impressed with it, because their personal character must necessarily influence that of their children, and be the source of their personal character. For, if the active performance of the duties of a citizen interfere, and it undoubtedly does so, with the duty of self-education, of what importance is it that men enter upon them with such a personal character as may insure us confidence while it secures us from temptation? The formation of such a character depends mainly on mothers, and especially on their personal character and principles. The character of the mother influences the children more than that of the father, because it is more exposed to their daily, hourly observation. It is difficult for these young, though acute observers, to comprehend the principles which regulate their father's political opinions; his vote in the senate; his conduct in political or commercial relations; but they can see,—yes! and they can estimate and imitate, the moral principles of the mother in her management of themselves, her treatment of her domestics, and the thousand petty details of the interior. These principles, whether lax or strict, low or high in moral tone, become, by an insensible and imperceptible adoption, their principles, and are carried out by them into the duties and avocations of future life. It would be startling to many to know with what intelligence and accuracy motives are penetrated, inconsistencies remarked, and treasured up with retributive or imitative projects, as may best suit the purpose of the moment. Nothing but a more extensive knowledge of children than is usually possessed on entering life, can awaken parents to the perception of this truth; and awakened perception may, perhaps, be only awakened misery. How important is it, then, that every thing in the education of women should tend to enlighten conscience, that she may enter on her arduous task with principles requiring only watchfulness, not reformation; and such a personal character as may exercise none but healthy influences on her children!

CHAPTER XI.

ON THE MEANS OF SECURING PERSONAL INFLUENCE.

Reverence in the child the future man.
Destroy not in the man the rudiments of an angel.
BARBAULD.

THE qualities which seem more especially needful in a character which is to influence others, are, consistency, simplicity, and benevolence, or love.

By consistency of character, I mean consistency of action with principle, of manner with thought, of *self* with *self*. The want of this quality is a failing with which our sex is often charged, and justly; but are we to blame? Our hearts are warm, our nerves irritable, and we have seen how little there is, in existing systems of female education, calculated to give wide, lofty, self-devoted principles of action. Without such principles, there can be no consistency of conduct; and without consistency of conduct, there can be no available moral influence.

The peculiar evil arising from want of consistency, is the want of trust or faith which it engenders. This is felt in the common intercourse with

9*

the world. In our relations with inconsistent persons, we are like mariners at sea without a compass. On the other hand, intercourse with consistent persons gives to the mind a sort of tranquillity, peculiarly favourable to happiness and to virtue. It is like the effect produced by the perception of an immutable truth, which, from the very force of contrast, is peculiarly grateful to the inhabitants of so changeable a world as this. It is moral repose.

This sort of moral repose is most peculiarly advantageous to children, because it allows ample scope for the developement of their mental and moral faculties; banishing from their minds all that chaotic bewilderment into which dependence on inconsistent persons throws them. It is advantageous to them in another, and more important way,—it prepares them for a belief in virtue; a trust in others, which it is easy to train up into a veneration for the source of all virtue; a trust in the origin of all truth. There can be no clearness of moral perception in the governed, where there is no manifestation of a moral rule of right in the governor. In speaking of moral perception, I do not mean to say that children have, properly speaking, a moral perception of inconsistency; but it affects their comfort and well-being, nevertheless. There is, in the nature of man, as great a perception of moral, as of physical order and proportion;

and the absence of the moral produces pain and disgust to the soul, as the absence of the physical does to the senses.   This state of pain and disgust is felt, though it can never be expressed, by children, who are under the management of inconsistent persons,—that is, persons whose conduct is guided solely by feeling, (good or bad,) by caprice, or impulse; and how injurious it is to them, we may easily conceive.   If, however, their present comfort only were endangered by it, the evil would be of comparatively small magnitude; but it affects their character for life.   They cease to trust, and they cease to venerate; now trust is the root of faith, and veneration of piety :—and when the root is destroyed, how can the plant flourish?   Perhaps we may remark that the effect here produced upon children is the same as that which long intercourse with the world produces in men: only that the effect differs in proportion to their differing intellectual faculties.   The child is annoyed, and knows not the cause of annoyance; the man is annoyed, and endeavours to lose the sense of discomfort in a universal scepticism as to human virtue, and a resolving of all actions into one principle, self-interest.   He thus seeks to create a principle possessing the stability which he desires, but seeks in vain to find; for, be it remembered, our love of moral stability is precisely as great as our love of physical change ;—another of the mys-

teries of our being.   The effects on the man are
the same as on the child,—he ceases to believe,
and he ceases to venerate; and the end is the most
degrading of all conditions,—the abnegation of all
abstract virtue, generosity, or love. Now, into this
state children are brought by the inconsistency of
parents,—that is, these young and innocent creatures are placed in a condition, moral and intellectual, which we consider an evil, even when produced by long contact with a selfish and unkind
world.   And thus they enter upon life, prepared
for vice in all its forms,—and scepticism, in all its
heart-withering tendencies.   How can parents
bear this responsibility ?   There is something so
touching in the simple faith of childhood,—its
utter dependence,—its willingness to believe in the
perfection of those to whom it looks for protection
—that to betray that faith, to shake that dependence, seems almost akin to irreligion.

The value of principle, then, in itself so precious,
is enhanced tenfold by constancy in its manifestations, and therefore consistency, as a source of influence, can never be too much insisted upon.

Consistency of principle is brought to the test in
every daily, hourly occurrence of woman's life, and
if she have been brought up without an abiding
sense of duty and responsibility, she is of all beings
most unfortunate; influences the most potent are
committed to her care, and from her they issue like

the simoom of the desert, breathing moral blight
and death.   I have endeavoured, in some degree,
to enforce the power of indirect influences on the
minds of *children :* they are very powerful in the
other relations of life ; in the conjugal, the truth
is too well known and attested by tale and song to
need additional corroboration here—and this book
is principally, though not wholly, dedicated to
woman in her maternal character.

The extreme importance of the manifestation of
consistency in mothers may be argued from this
fact, that it is of infinite importance to children to
see the daily operation of an immutable and consistent rule of right, in matters sufficiently small
to come within the sphere of childish observation, and, therefore, if called upon to give a defi-
nition of the peculiar mission of woman, and the
peculiar source of her influence, I should say it
is the application of large principles to small
duties,—the agency of comprehensive intelligence on details.   That largeness of mental vision, which, while it can comprehend the vast, is
too keen to overlook the little, is especially to be
cultivated by women.   It is a great mistake to
suppose the two qualities are incompatible, and
the supposition that they are so, has done much
mischief; the error arises not from the extent, but
from the narrowness of our capacity.   *To aspire* is
our privilege, and a privilege which we are by no

means slack to use, without considering that the
operations of infinitude are even more incomprehensible in their minuteness than in their magnitude, and that, therefore, to be always looking from
the minute towards the vast, is only a proof of the
finite nature of our present capacity.   The loftiest
intellect may, without abasement, be employed on
the minutest domestic detail, and in all probability
will perform it better than an inferior one ; it is
the motive and end of an action which makes it
either dignified or mean.   In the homely words
of old Herbert,

> All may of thee partake :
> Nothing can be so mean,
> Which with this tincture, *for thy sake*
> Will not grow bright and clean.

It is then in the minutiæ of daily life and conduct that this consistency has its most beneficial
operation, and it must derive its power from the
personal character for this reason, that no virtues
but indigenous ones are capable of the sort of
moral transfusion here mentioned.   It is rare to
see a parent eminently distinguished by any moral
virtue, unsuccessful in transmitting that virtue to
children, simply because, being an integral part of
character, it is consistent in its mode of operation ;
so virtues originating in effort, or practised for the
sake of example, are seldom transferable ; the same

consistency cannot be expected in the exercise of them, and this may explain the small success of pattern mothers, *par excellence* so called, and whose good intentions and sacrifices ought not to be objects of derision; the very appearance of effort mars the effect of all effort.

The world is sometimes surprised to see extraordinary proofs of moral influence exercised by persons who never planned, never aimed, to obtain such influence,—nay, whose conduct is never regulated by any fixed aim for its attainment; the fact is, that those characters are composed of truth and love;—truth, which prevents the assumption even of virtues which are not natural, thereby adding to the influence of such as are; love, the most contagious of all moral contagions, the regenerating principle of the world!

The virtue which mainly contributes to the support of consistency—without which, in fact, consistency cannot exist—is simplicity; consistency of conduct can never be maintained by characters in any degree double or sophisticated, for it is not of simplicity as opposed to craft, but of simplicity as opposed to sophistication, that I would here speak, and rather as the Christian virtue, single-mindedness; the desire to *be*, opposed to the wish to *appear*. We have seen how rarely influence can be gained where no faith can be yielded; now an unsimple character can never inspire faith or trust

People do not always analyze mental phenomena sufficiently to know the reason of this fact, but no one will dispute the fact itself. It is true there are persons who have the power of conciliating confidence of which they are unworthy, but it is only because (like Castruccio Castrucciani) they are such exquisite dissemblers, that their affectation of simplicity has temporarily the effect of simplicity itself. This power of successful assumption is, fortunately, confined to very few, and the pretenders to unreal virtues and the utterer of assumed sentiments are only ill-paid labourers, working hard to reap no harvest-fruits.

An objection slightly advanced before, may here naturally occur again, and may be answered more fully, viz: the opposition of the conventional forms of society to entire simplicity of thought and action, and consequently to influence. The influence which conventionalism has over principle is to be utterly disclaimed, but its having an injurious influence over manner is far more easily obviated; so easily, indeed, that it may be doubted whether there be not more simplicity in compliance than in opposition. Originality, either of thought or behaviour, is most uncommon, and only found in minds above, or in minds below, the ordinary standard; neither is this peculiar feature of society in itself a blame-worthy one: it arises out of the constitution of man, naturally imitative, gregarious,

nd desirous of approbation. Nothing would be
ained by the abolition of these forms, for they are
epresentatiyes of a good spirit; the spirit, it is
·ue, is too often not there, but it would be better
› call it back than to abolish the form. We have
n opportunity of judging how far it would be con-
enient or agreeable to do so, in the conduct of
›me *soi-disant* contemners of forms; we perceive
ıat such contempt is equally the offspring of self-
hness with slavish regard : it is only the exchange
f the selfishness of vanity for the selfishness of in-
olence and pride, and the world is the loser by
ıe exchange. Hypocrisy has been said to be the
omage which vice pays to virtue. Conventional
›rms may, with justice, be called the homage
·hich selfishness pays to benevolence.

How then is simplicity of character to be pre-
·rved without violating conventionalism, to which
seems so much at variance, and yet, which it
ıght not to oppose? By the cultivation of that
»irit of which conventional forms are only the
·mbol, by training children in the early exercise of
ıe kind and benevolent affections, and by exacting
. the domestic circle all those observances which
·e the signs of good will in society, so that they may
? the emanations of a benevolent heart, instead of
ıe gloss of artificial politeness. Conventionalism
ill never injure the simplicity of such characters
ı these, nay, it may greatly add to their influence,

10

and secure for their virtues and talents the reception that they deserve; it is a part of benevolence to cultivate the graces that may persuade or allure men to the imitation of what is right. " Stand off, I am holier than thou," is not more foreign to true piety, than " stand off, I am wiser than thou," is to true benevolence, as relates to those " things indifferent," in which we are told that we may be all things to all men.

The cultivation of domestic politeness is a subject not nearly enough attended to, yet it is the sign, and ought to be the manifestation, of many beautiful virtues—affection, self-denial, elegance, are all called into play by it; and it has a potent recommendation in its being an excellent preservative against affectation, which generally arises from a great desire to please, joined to an ignorance of the means of pleasing successfully. It is to be hoped that these remarks will not be deemed trifling or irrelevant in a chapter on the means of securing personal influence. Powers of pleasing are a very great source of that influence, and there is no telling how great might be the benefit to society, if all on whom they are bestowed (and how lavishly they are bestowed on woman!) would be persuaded to use them, not as a means of selfish gratification, but as an engine for the promotion of good.* Such

* It was a beautiful idea in the mythology of the ancients, which identified the Graces with the Charities of social life.

wers are as sacred a trust from the Creator as
y other gift, and ought to be equally used for his
ry, and the advancement of moral good. Vir-
:, indeed, in itself is venerable, but it must be
ractive in order to be influential. And how at-
.ctive it might be, if the powers of pleasing,
lich can cover and even recommend the deform-
of vice, were conscientiously excited in its be-
lf! This is the peculiar province of women,
d they are peculiarly fitted for it by Nature.
ieir personal loveliness, their versatile powers,
d lively fancy, qualify them in an eminent de-
ee to adorn, and by adorning to recommend,
·tue and religion.

Cosi all' egro fanciul porgiamo aspersi
Di soave licor gli orli del vaso,

CHAPTER XII.

ON THE MEANS OF SECURING PERSONAL INFLUENCE.—(*Continued.*)

Domestic happiness, thou only bliss
Of Paradise, that has survived the fall!
Though few now taste thee unimpaired and pure,
Or tasting, long enjoy thee! too infirm,
Or too incautious, to preserve thy sweets
Unmixed with drops of bitter, which neglect
Or temper sheds into thy crystal cup.
Thou art the nurse of virtue, in thine arms
She smiles, appearing, as in truth she is,
Heaven-born, and destined to the skies again.

COWPER.

CONSISTENCY and simplicity bear yet in anothe
and a very important point of view upon persona
influence, consequently upon woman's usefulness
They are opposed, in the highest degree, to exag
geration of sentiment, to which the excitable imagi
nations and ardent feelings of women render then
particularly prone.   This is sometimes most pain
fully illustrated in the case of the gifted of ou
sex; for the extent of their reasoning capacity i
not always commensurate with the intense vivaci
ty of the perceptive, and the consequent want o
common sense displayed by them has furnishe

great occasion for ridicule.   Thus women have
armed men with a weapon against themselves. In
using this weapon, they have evinced some skill,
but little honesty, for till they have proved that the
eccentricity is *caused* by the superiority, they have
proved nothing ; the fact is, that it is a defect inci-
dent to the nature of women's minds, which nothing
in their education has a tendency to bias.   It has
been urged that the first point in the education of
women, is the cultivation of the heart and the affections ; the second, is that of the judgment.   It is of
the utmost consequence that they join a calm and
penetrating judgment to a warm heart and lively
imagination, else their very virtues may be the
means of leading them astray.   They want that
spirit of worldly-minded prudence and calculation
which often supplies to men the deficiency of the
reasoning faculty, (for it is surprising how good a
logician is self-interest,) and consequently entail
upon themselves that character of fickleness and
infirmness of purpose with which men in all ages
have reproached them.

We will not here stop to settle the relative de-
grees of merit between vacillation arising from
weakness of head, and firmness which springs from
coldness of heart ; but only urge upon women, as
they value their influence, to shake off this reproach.   Nay, if the reproach were the extent of
the evil, we might rejoice ; but exaggeration of
10*

sentiment is the occasion of other and more serious
evils.   It has a tendency to transfer to the head,
as a fancy, what ought to be lodged in the heart
as a principle.   Now, fancy is proverbially fickle
and changeable, and a succession of fancies must
be injurious to consistency and dignity of character, consequently to influence.   Good sentiments
seated in the imagination, are to good principles
lodged in the heart, what the house, founded upon
the sand, is to the house founded upon the rock, and
the stability of them is just as doubtful.   The first
shock unsettles them, the first tempest overturns
them, and it is not till we see the extent of the ruins
that we perceive how utterly baseless was the fabric.

Exaggeration of sentiment has, too, another
danger; it is apt to produce a kind of moral epi-
curism very fatal to character; a luxuriating in the
possession of exalted moral sentiments; a self-complacency in their indulgence.   It too often happens
that the deceived heart, lulled into false security
by the self-gratulation thus engendered, forgets the
bearing of the speculative on the practical, and adds
to very high-flying speculation very low-creeping
practice.   It is easy for a mind in this state to
argue itself into acquiescence in any opinions which
do not alarm the sense of self-complacency.   In
order that it be not alarmed, it is only necessary
that an evil principle be clothed with the garb of
an " angel of light," and a welcome and a willing

reception await the flattering guest. Once received, it prepares the way for another and another, till the mind, losing all equipoise, is left in a bewilderment of folly and sophistication, conscious of error, yet unable to extricate itself—a moral chaos !

The remedy for these evils, to which all persons, especially women, are exposed, is the implanting of broad and deep fundamental principles of action, and the cultivation of the reasoning powers. If it be objected that expansion of mind will unfit women for their minute and peculiar duties, it may be answered that the objection is no less unphilo-sophical than false. Do we not see the electric fluid, which shakes the spheres, operating upon the growth of the meanest plant ? Are not the mathe-matical truths which guided Newton in the disco-very of the solar system, available to the child in the construction of his Chinese puzzle ? It is ri-diculous to talk of extension occasioning imperfec-tion ; in falsehood, indeed, extension of limit only adds to extension of error, but a fundamental truth is to be recognised by its powers of infinite and universal application. It is not because women's powers have been cultivated and enlarged, that they overlook their minute duties, but because they have been only partially cultivated and en-larged in a wrong direction.* There is no cause

[* This is a sound distinction, and of the very first importance.]

to dread that expansion of mind will lead to neglect
of minor and proximate duties.   That is the peculiar danger of exaggeration of sentiment, against
which expansion of mind is proposed as a defence.
Exaggeration of sentiment, even when inclined to
the side of virtue, has a false foundation ; and we
have seen, that no principle, not fundamentally
true, can be trusted in unlimited operation.   The
reasoning power will show us that we can, in no
degree, compensate to society for the neglect of
those duties that lie nearest us ; or secure peace to
our own minds, except by the performance of
them.   "Do the duty that lies nearest thee," says
the German sage.   Oh ! that we could all make
this the motto of our heart and of our life, and do
the. duty that lies nearest us with all our heart,
and all our mind, and all our soul, and all our
strength.

And here I would address myself to the educators
of female youth, beseeching them to consider the
deep importance of their occupation,—entreating
them to remember that to them is intrusted the
training of beings whose mission on earth is not
only to shine, to please, to adorn, but to influence,
and, by influencing, to regenerate ;—that the chief
object of their education is not so much to fit them
to adorn society, as to vivify and enlighten a home.
What a paradise even this world might become, if
one half the amount of effort expended in vain

attempts to excite the admiration of strangers, were reserved to vary the amusements and adorn the sacred precincts of home! Here is an inexhaustible field of effort, and inexhaustible source of happiness: and here women are the undoubted agents, and they complain of having no scope for exertion! The happiness without which wealth, honours, nay, intellectual pleasures, are but gilded toys, it is theirs to produce and foster: and they have no mission! The only bliss of Paradise that has survived the fall, is deposited in their keeping, and they have no importance; alas! for the mental vision of those who see not the things that belong unto their own peace and the peace of others.

No one will think these remarks superfluous who is conscious how little effort is ever expended in the adornment of a home. Do we not constantly see women before marriage, lovely, accomplished, radiant with smiles and fashion, sinking into homely household managers, or at best insipidly good-natured companions, in the very homes which perhaps these qualities may have procured for them? Do we not see daughters on whom parents have lavished expense, refusing to exert, for the amusement of those parents, the very acquirements which they have procured for them? A stranger enters,—the scene changes; smiles, graces, accomplishments, are lavished upon him. It is a sicken-

ing scene, and the finest of satires on the so-called
education of the young. Till the philosophy of
domestic happiness has undergone a thorough reformation, let not women seek to invade the sphere
of the other sex; or we may safely allow those
only to do so who can say with truth, that for the
comfort, the elegance, the happiness of the home
of which they are the tutelary divinities, nothing
remains to be done ; till home, instead of being a
scene of vapid indifference, perhaps of angry con-
tention, is the Elysium of each and all of its
sharers,—the favourite field for the exercise of
virtues,—the favourite scene of display for graces
and accomplishments.

This subject has been particularly insisted upon
because the spirit of the times seems particularly
to require it. The world is in a state of philan-
thropic Quixotism (and it is a very good sign of
the world); but before we go forth with lance and
shield to assist all manner of distress, let us look
well to ourselves, and see that by our absence and
neglect other objects are not added to the distressed
needing succour. May we not with reason urge
upon our own sex, that, as the philosophy of domestic happiness is in a state so little advanced,
it affords a fine field for the energies and talents
which they are so desirous of rendering available
to the community ?

CHAPTER XIII.

THE MISSIONARY SPIRIT.

Some there are
By their good works exalted, lofty minds,
And meditative authors of delight
And happiness, which to the end of time
Will live, and spread, and kindle.
WORDSWORTH.

missionary spirit. These words, often abused,
ı misconceived, have yet a deep meaning. To
ɔver that meaning, to rectify that misconcep-
is the first object of this chapter; to apply
ı with truth and force to our subject, the se-
l. They comprehend, to my mind, all that the
ld has that is noble and pure,—the triumph of
ıeavenly over the earthly part of our nature,—
reign of love! It will soon be seen how and
re, with these views of it, I conceive it to bear
ı our subject.

n attentive survey of the world around us will
Ꞌe to the most careless observer that it is divided,
shades and minor subdivisions being infinite,)
two distinct classes: those who live for them-
ᴇs, and those who live for something out of

themselves. The principal objects of the first class are worldly and tangible—those of the other are unworldly and ideal. This is not assuming that all worth, or all usefulness, is on the side of idealism : it is only drawing a distinction, which no one will refuse to admit ;—nay, it must be allowed that the worldly spirit is a very needful agent in driving on the physical well-being of society. Concession must stop here ; for if we talk of *ennobling the species*, that spirit is plainly not intended for this end ; for it seems that, in exact proportion to its subjugation, our nature assumes the highest perfection of which it is here capable, and (we say it with reverence,) to approach more nearly to that perfection of which all earthly excellence is but the type and shadow. The manifestations of the unworldly spirit are not always watched and prized as they ought to be ; for, like every other good gift, it loses somewhat of its value by being committed to earthen vessels, and often assumes forms so little corresponding with its intrinsic value, that it loses its deserved estimation. Nay, it is so little akin to the world and its ways, that the possessors of it are too often objects of reproach and derision. Nor is all the blame here on the side of the world ; persons professing to act in opposition to its ordinary rules and maxims, should take up the tone of conciliation, not of defiance,—of explanation, not of mystery. The consciousness of being above the world, ought to increase, not lessen, our love and charity to those that are in it. What are the words of the greatest of missionaries,—the most devoted to man's interests,—the most self-sacrificing of all the apostles:—" I would be all things to all men, that I may by all means save some." " To be good and disagreeable is high treason against virtue." And if the world is sometimes prone to call evil good, and good evil, we must allow that the champions of the good provoke it to do so, by taking up an offensive position, instead of marching forward under the banner of the " Prince of Peace."

It is not from narrow prejudice, or from ascetic and bigoted views, that such frequent strictures have been made in this book on the utilitarian philosophy ; but from an honest conviction that the best and highest interests of man are thereby compromised. No candid person will refuse to admit that, for some reason or the other, inscrutable to us, the increase and perfecting of physical improvements has a tendency to concentrate the thoughts of man upon self. Is it because the more exquisite perception of the glories of this world shut out from us the remembrance that we were born for a still nobler and better ? Strange inconsistency ! that the very enlargement of the means of vision should shut out the extent of the view. Strange ! that the creature should be prone to

11

forget the Creator in the very discoveries which he daily makes of his power and his goodness. How can it be, that this manifestation of love in one being, brings forth the manifestation of selfishness in another? They who in thought ponder on these things, will not deny the truth of what is here asserted; and it is a most curious exercise of ingenuity to account for such extraordinary phenomena of the human mind.

The besetting sin of our age is a kind of epicurean selfishness. An increased value of physical enjoyment, a kind of material atmosphere, engendered by the stupendous progress of physical science, produces a rooted, though unavowed, scepticism, as to the value of the unseen and ideal. The love of life crushes the belief of that most important of all truths, that there are things more valuable than life itself. The lofty indifference to mere physical enjoyment; the preference of others to ourselves; of the unseen to the present; of the ideal to the tangible; which, where they do exist, attest the strivings of the divinity within us: where will they soon be? Yet, so completely does the Divinity oppose the infringement of his laws, that they, and they only, are happy people, who do live for the ideal. He seems to take pleasure in asserting the superiority of his works, by not allowing its noblest and purest reflections of himself to be *obscured* by intervening shadows. It is the fashion to sneer at those *ideas*, for which men in different ages have suffered toil, pain, privation, death: the object might be wild—the recovery of a shrine: weak—the love of a woman; untrue, (if we are to believe the infidel,)—the announcement of a world beyond the grave! Be it so: poor victims of idiosyncracy! they sacrificed all tangible and solid benefits for a vapour. But who are they, at whose names the eye flashes and the cheek colours, whose memories leave behind them a train of light, like a glorious departing orb? The successful speculator; the luxurious epicurean; the wealthy; the worldly?—no: the oppressed but dauntless victim of tyranny; the devoted, though perhaps mistaken, sufferer for fantastic loyalty; the agonized martyr to truth. And for personal happiness, let one of the foremost of these victims of idiosyncracy speak for himself, in his own noble words,—" We are troubled on every side, but not distressed; we are perplexed, but not in despair; persecuted, but not forsaken; cast down, but not destroyed:" and contrast them with the mournful confession of him, who, having exhausted all that this world has to bestow,—honour, glory, power, wealth,—bequeathed to us, as the melancholy result of his experience, that they were " altogether vanity."

The missionary spirit is neither more nor less than the direction of this ideality into its best and noblest channels. It is the union of two qualities which are necessary in the moral regeneration of our race. The character of the ideal is, indeed, noble in its postponement of self, but it must be useful likewise, before we have the missionary spirit. In a word, love must be added to unselfishness: it must not be passive and unresisting, but active and enduring unselfishness; not simply the going out of self, but the going into others,—the imitation, as far as human nature allows, of that divine perfection of love, whose bliss must be in blessing. The spirit may, in some degree, be acquired by cultivation; but there is one natural manifestation of it, and that is placed in woman's heart,—maternal love,—the only purely unselfish feeling that exists on this earth; the only affection which (as far as it appears,) flows from the loving to the beloved object in one continual stream, uninterrupted by those impediments which check every other. Disease, deformity, ingratitude,— nothing can check the flow of maternal love. By intrusting to woman such a revelation of himself, God has pointed out whom he intends for his missionaries upon earth,—the disseminators of his spirit, the diffusers of his word. Let men enjoy in peace and triumph the intellectual kingdom which is theirs, and which doubtless was intended for them; let us participate its privileges, without desiring to share its dominion. The moral world *is ours*,—ours by position; ours by qualification;

ours by the very indication of God himself, who
has deigned to place in woman's heart the only
feeling, (that we know of, here existing,) which
affords the faintest representation of his most unextinguishable love to us, his erring and strayed
children; the only affection which enables the
possessor to love on through sin and folly; and
even when sin and folly have brought their last,
worst, consummation.

Oh! those who know, those who have witnessed
the lingering yearning of a mother's love, after one
lost in crime, and wandering, and ingratitude;
when even the father's heart was turned to stone;
the unextinguished, unextinguishable sentiment,
lighting up even the dying eye, and breathed forth
in the dying prayer, can alone judge of these things.
Who that has witnessed these scenes, (and how
many have witnessed them whom the world thinks
happy!) can doubt where the regenerating principle lies,—can doubt that it is in the sex which is
permitted to be the depository of a feeling so typi-
cal of the Divine love!

This language is warm; it comes from the
heart; it is not therefore to be thought exaggerated. It comes from the understanding also: it is
only the energetic expression of a sober conviction
formed from a long series of observation.

But women who are not mothers have a mission
likewise. The germs of that holy love are in them

11*

also ; they need only to be cherished and expended on other subjects.   Their mission is the establishment of peace, and love; and unselfishness, to be achieved by any means, and at any cost to themselves ; in the cultivation first in themselves, then in all over whom they have any influence, of an unselfish and unworldly spirit ; the promotion even in the most minute particular of elegance, of happiness, of moral good.   The poor, the ignorant, the domestic servant, are their children ; and on them let them lavish the love which God has denied to flow in its natural channel.   In any way—in every way—in which God and man can be served, it is theirs to serve, gracefully, peaceably, unostentatiously.   And for happiness—let them not doubt of it ; it shall be theirs to understand the depth of the " peace which passeth all understanding ;" the accordance, that is, of the divine and human will. God points the way, let his missionaries follow ; it is his cause ; it is the cause of human nature ; it is the cause of souls destined for immortality, and which ask their birthright at our hands !

CHAPTER XIV.

RELIGION.

Quel spectacle plus effrayant que celui d'un peuple actif et vigoureux, se débattant sans espérance dans les murs d'airain et de la fausse gloire, de la personalité et de l'égoisme. Ce spectacle nous le donnons au monde, parceque la pensée religieuse nous manque ; et la pensée religieuse nous manque parceque les mères ont oublié de la déposer sur le berceau de leurs enfans.

AIME MARTIN.

IT remains yet to discover the main-spring of all those qualities which have been so strenuously insisted upon as necessary to direct the undisputed influence of women into its right channel. In the state to which we have brought the argument, it is liable to the objection that it enforces the necessity of impossible and unattainable virtue. The qualities recommended as most essential to secure woman's influence, are indeed, as yet, plants without roots : for how can *they* regenerate society who are not themselves regenerate ? who have not " the spirit which cometh from God only ?" There is but one source of regeneration, and that is Christianity : the women, therefore, who are to be regenerators of society, must be women deeply imbued with the spirit of Christianity ; the spirit, not the letter, —for I would not here speak of forms, however venerable, or dogmas, however important, but of that complete surrender of heart to the cause of God, and the promotion of his glory, which is the essence of Christianity. It is of the utmost consequence that all be instructed on this point, for Christianity has too long, and too exclusively, been regarded as a scheme of redemption, and not enough as a scheme of regeneration. Is it too bold to assert, that the principal proof of its value, as a redemption, is its power of regeneration? for if it only promised us an entrance into a state of holiness and happiness, for which it had no evident tendency to prepare us, we might be almost excused for doubting the existence of that state, and the value of the redemption which is promised.

On the internal and intrinsic evidences of Christianity, theological writers and preachers do not ever sufficiently insist. Its exquisite adaptation to our state and faculties, its enlarged and progressive tendencies, above all, the matchless perfection of the divine model proposed for our imitation— these obtain only cursory and partial attention, while the discussions on inferior matters of the law, the tithe of mint and cummin, perplex, and alas ! shake the Christian world. When we see how completely these things contain within themselves solutions of difficulties otherwise unsolvable,—materials for happiness confessedly unattainable by earthly blessings, and undiscoverable by human wisdom,—moral truths so new and startling, that their first announcement must have occasioned the greatest surprise, yet so meeting difficulties as to receive immediate acquiescence,— we are quite ready to exclaim, this is, indeed, a system come from God. This subject, however, in its magnitude, is too vast for the limits of this work, and the abilities of the writer, who has only entered upon it with a view of singling out a few truths bearing with peculiar force upon the subjects discussed in this book.

The first of these truths is, that Christianity is the only scheme which has annexed happiness to self-renunciation, and thus made a revelation of our true and real nature, and the nature of the state to which we are tending. It is true that self-renunciation from patriotic motives was recommended and enforced by ancient sages and legislators, but the reward annexed was glory, not happiness. The heathens had patriotism, but not philanthropy; they loved their fellow-citizens, not their fellow-men; they lived before we were taught to know God as *our* Father. This doctrine of self-renunciation, as a source of happiness, is at first very surprising, and must be entirely so to an unchristian spirit, because it is in direct opposition to the natural impulses of the human heart, which are

mostly selfish. Yet we can perceive how prób
it would be that such a doctrine must be the
one, by the fact that it approximates us most ne
to that glorious Being who, as he is infinitely b
volent, must be infinitely happy. We shall be
further convinced, if we take the trouble to
sider what are the principal sources of miser
the world. They are pride and self-opinion,
ity, and covetousness. What are all these v
but exhibitions, under different forms, of the se
principle? All the petty differences, and pa
contentions, which arise from these passions,
the efforts of the selfish principle for its own gra
cation. If this principle were but once banis
from the world, (where, alas! it reigns but
paramount,) how light comparatively would be
burden of evil which, for our perfecting, we r
all bear, but which, however it may cause the f
to mourn, need never destroy the peace w
passeth all understanding, the calm heart of fa

Blessed are the poor in spirit: what an inex
cable annunciation! How mean! says the sce
How grand! says the Christian. The poverty u
which the blessing is here pronounced, is n
feeling of degradation, but of aspiration. It is
earnest of futurity,—our patent of nobility!
are poor in spirit *here*, because we would be
sons of God *hereafter ;* because we are permi
to view and love the holiness, which we feel

inability to reach. This poverty of spirit is one
modification of unselfishness, and the root of it is
love to God; the fruits of it will be love likewise,
—love to man,—and love produces self-forgetfulness, and self-forgetfulness produces happiness.
Here we have a fact accounted for, and a mystery
solved. The fact is undoubted, and so generally
acknowledged, that a reference to it seems almost
too trite and common. It is the manifest insuffi-
ciency of worldly blessings for the production of
happiness—because they are a gratification of the
selfish principle. Earthly and animal enjoyment
is an unspeakably benevolent boon of the Creator;
but not, in itself, happiness. Happiness, properly
so called, is only to be found, as has before been
shown, in the accordance of the divine and human
will; in the exercise, then, of those faculties of the
soul by which we are approximated to the divinity. Happiness, therefore, must derive its source
from the unselfish principle; a proof that, however degraded our nature may be, it still retains
the impress of Him " who made man in his own
image." What are acknowledged to be the purest
sources of felicity here below ?—The affections.
And what are the affections but unselfishness?
Oh ! why are these pure and holy sources of felicity so little cultivated, so little understood, as
means not only of enjoyment, but of moral rene-
vation. Why do we, by our unregenerate tempers

and paltry selfishness, so often turn to bitter this one drop of unalloyed sweetness that is mingled with the draught of life?

The mystery solved is no less a one than that of our being,—we are not destined to terminate our course here. We are only here preparatory to our introduction to a higher scene,—a scene of virtue, of unselfishness, of love. This view of the case cannot be too much impressed upon our minds, for it has been grievously warped by prejudice and bigotry. This world is not a world of trial only, but a world of *preparation*. What does the word *preparation* mean?—A storing up of things with a view to future exigencies. The folly of that traveller would excite surprise who should enter a foreign country unprepared with language or current coin; and yet men think that by some process resembling an experiment in alchemy, they shall gain admittance into heaven, with earthly passions boiling in their hearts, and worldly motives influencing their conduct. The choleric, the vindictive, the selfish, kneel, and with upraised eyes implore admission into the heaven, and the presence of the God of love! What should they do there? What reason have they to hope that the God of mercy and benevolence can so far forget his nature as to look with complacency on *them?* God is love, and we can have no sure ground for *hope that* we are objects of his favour here, or that we shall be admitted to his presence hereafter, if we neglect to cultivate that spirit which he has deigned to call his own; by enjoining the imitation of which he has intended to secure, not only our happiness *here*, but *hereafter*,—our happiness *here*, *because* it is to be our happiness hereafter. The very foundations of our faith are all developements of this principle. The voluntary humiliation of one, who, " though he was rich, yet for our sakes became poor,"—the sufferings of the sinless for the sinful,—the life of privation,—the death of ignominy,—what are all these but living and breathing testimonials that God is love? What ought they to announce to all, but that till the same spirit prevail in the world the "good tidings of great joy" have come, but are not received or understood; that peace, though proclaimed, is not ratified?

We are told, that till we are rooted and grounded in love, we cannot comprehend the height and depth of holy things,* and for this reason we see such lamentable shipwreck made of Christian charity, by many who would be shocked to be suspected of any want of Christian faith. The

[* " That ye, *being rooted and grounded in love, may be able* to comprehend with all saints what is the breadth, and length, and depth, and height, and *to know the love of Christ.*" (St. Paul to the Ephesians.)—To experience and enjoy the love of Christ, we must have loving hearts. " Love is the fulfilling of the law."]

Gospel is a sealed book to them—sealed, at least, as to its most divine properties, and this is the reason why Christianity, so ample in its proofs of divine origin, so adapted to the wants and weaknesses of our nature, has not yet worked its perfect work upon our globe. Men have been scanning it with the intellect, and not with the heart! what wonder is it, then, that a system addressed to the heart, and intended to operate upon the heart, has eluded their researches! How are they repaid for these researches? by unbelief, which makes them objects of compassion, not of blame. What is there in the conduct of the generality of professing Christians which tends to rectify their errors? When we see that glorious and holy book—which ought to be the treasury of the good things of peace, and hope, and joy—used, even by those who profess to value it, as an armoury to which they resort for weapons of offence; when we hear men loudly and boldly declaiming concerning the hidden purposes of God, as though they had secret intimation of them, calling down on any, and on whom they will, his eternal wrath, and clothing the Deity with their own bad passions and selfish dispositions, we are ready to lift our eyes and ask, where sleep thy thunderbolts?* Christians themselves

[* Just what we ought not to ask. " Father forgive them, for they know not what they do."]

put arms into the hands of their opponents, and what right have they to complain of the wounds which they receive? But we may beseech the sceptic to recollect that till he can find in that blessed book—one maxim of selfishness—one trait of malevolence—one *word* which can authorize the bad and unholy passions which, clothed in the garb of religion, have desolated society, he has no right to charge upon the system the errors of those who embrace it—who profess to embrace it, I should say, for, assuredly, such persons know as little of Christianity as the uninstructed heathen. They are very ready with the charge of blasphemy —we may ask who are the true blasphemers, but they who clothe the religion of the Father who loved us, and the Saviour who died for us, in such a frightful garb of human folly and wickedness, that its very nature is changed and distorted, and it stands—a mark of derision to the infidel and the scorner. If any proof be needed—how " far we are gone from original righteousness," it is indeed a lamentable one, that a system so worthy of God, and so adapted to our state and nature, has been so long proclaimed, and found so faint an echo in human hearts.

" It is now high time to awake out of sleep," and to proclaim Christianity what it is,—the destined instrument, not only of our redemption. but of our regeneration; and let it never be forgotten—*only* of our redemption, so far as it is our regeneration.* Let all the glosses which induce men to believe themselves Christians vanish before this truth—that there is no proof of a right to Christian hopes, but the possession of a Christian spirit—and before the tremendous denunciation of our Lord: "Then will I say unto them in that day, Depart from me, I have never known ye !"

The want of this Christian spirit, so inexplicable in all who profess to take the Gospel for their guide, is peculiarly obnoxious in women so professing, for it is not only foreign to the nature of their religion, but foreign to their own nature. What was the reason that so many women were among the first converts to Christianity ? Because those pure and loving and self-denying doctrines found a ready echo in woman's heart. It seems to be particularly a part of women's mission to exhibit Christianity in its beauty and purity, and to disseminate it by example and culture. They have the greatest advantages afforded to them for the fulfilment of this mission, and are under the greatest obligations to fulfil it. For woman never would, and never could have risen to her present station in the social system, had it not been for the dignity with which Christianity invested those qualities,

[* "Jesus Christ gave himself for us, that he might *redeem us from all iniquity*, and purify unto himself a peculiar people, *zealous of good works*."]

peculiarly her own—no human eye could thus have seen into the deep things of God—no human penetration could have discovered the counsel of Him who has chosen the weak things of this world to confound the strong! No human wisdom could have discovered that pride is not strength, nor self-opinion greatness of soul—nor bravery, sublimity—nor glory, happiness—and that our highest honour, as creatures, is submission; as sinners, humility; as brethren, love. This revelation at once settled the condition of woman, by exalting her own peculiar qualities in the moral grade. It is true that ancient Greece and Rome showed in their institutions some respect for women, and some sense of their influence; but how?—by striving to endow them with masculine virtues. Men honoured them with reference to themselves, and only as far as they resembled themselves, and forgot the gentleness, lowliness, and humility proper to their sex—as *women:* and consequently—as *inferiors*, they were despised. No! Christianity brought to light the true value of women, by proclaiming the reign of love and unselfishness; and women, (alas! that there are such,) who despise and deny the Gospel, are slaves who trample on their charter of manumission. The system which has placed the seat of virtue in the heart, and equalized the value of great and small duties by referring every thing to motive, takes away at once all pre-

12*

tence of scorn for woman, on account of her inferior
social position and limited sphere of action. It
sheds its light no less on her sequestered path, than
on man's public way, and shows that they equally
lead to heaven—with this difference, that if his is
the more honourable, hers is the more secure.
Christianity once received—the condition of women is ascertained never to be altered; they, equally
with man, are denizens of heaven; they, equally
with man, have received the spirit of adoption,
whereby they cry, Abba Father! What a deep
meaning is hidden in those words—peculiarly
touching to woman, since they proclaim her no
longer the slave of man, but the servant of God.
Can women be anything but Christians, when they
hear the scornful thanksgiving of the Jew, that he
was not born a woman—when they read in the
creed of Mahomet that their highest destiny in the
next world, (even if they enter it,) is to minister to
the passions of which they were the slaves in this
—when they think that in humane Greece and
polished Rome, woman was only honoured as she
bore citizens to the commonwealth, and as she
could look with tearless eye on the slaughter of the
husband or the son, whom God had given her to
love and to cherish. Let them turn to the pages of
Scripture, and see the compassionate Jesus, consoling the sisters of Lazarus—addressing the daughters
of Jerusalem—commending his mother to the loved

disciple—and ask their own hearts whence they derive light, freedom, and privileges, not granted by scornful condescension, or held by precarious tenure, but secured to them as a right, by the unerring fiat of the Son of God!

But benefits are not to make us rejoice only, they ought to make us grateful. Extension of privilege is only extension of responsibility, and when not so considered, is a bane, not a blessing, to the privileged. If we are sensible of the benefits conferred upon us by our share in this great redemption, what ought to be our conduct? The adoption into our hearts, and the dissemination, by our influence, of this most holy spirit of Christianity; not with ostentatious profession and declamation, but with silent and vigilant agency. If it be true, generally, that "the kingdom of God cometh not with observation," it is more particularly true of woman's share in that great work. Religion, like every other good thing, loses its influence, if once it can be suspected that it is used as a medium of display. There is a kind of quiet consistency of conduct in truly Christian people, which begins by exciting wonder, and ends by securing respect. It is very puzzling to a selfish and worldly mind to see the action of an immutable principle of right as frequently operating *against* the worldly interests of the individual as not. This is the peculiar form of Christianity which we, as women, ought to cultivate, and till it is more generally cultivated, our religion will never be displayed in its real loveliness. Christian virtues, in this form, are more easy of practice to women than to men, because women have fewer worldly interests, and are by nature and education less selfish. The opportunities of reflection and self-communion which they enjoy, too, are more frequent, and these especially contribute to the support of consistency of conduct, which has been shown to be of such vast importance to woman's beneficial influence. In fact, it seems as though no other principles or motives could be found sufficiently powerful to insure it. When we consider the spirit of self-renunciation requisite for the maintenance of consistency, and for ensuring woman's influence, if we turn not to Christianity, where else can we look for it? The chief difference between native good feeling and abiding good principle is this, that the one is fitful and capricious in its operation; the other, constant and invariable. Reverence to God, and a vivid perception of his greatness and attributes, may, it is true, exist in minds not enlightened by Christian truth. A certain desire to love and serve him may also exist, but where is the law that teaches us how to do so—is it written on our hearts? Turn to the human sacrifices of antiquity; to the self-inflicted tortures of the Brahmin; to the declaration of Socrates, that unless heaven should deign

to make a special revelation, man must ever remain
in ignorance of God's nature, and the means of
conciliating his favour. Turn, likewise, to the
ages when the Bible was shut up from the world,
(professedly Christian,) yet, having so little of the
Christian spirit, that the war of the Albigenses
was a holy crusade, and the mercy of God was
represented by the fires of the inquisition. For let
it never be forgotten, that Christians are bound
to disclaim, in the name of their religion, such
tortuous indications of religious feeling. What
does the Bible say to all this? "Be not wise in
your own conceits." "Who art thou that judgest
another man's servant? To his own master he
standeth or falleth." Why will we not go to the
Bible, not only for our rule of faith, but for our
rule of life, for the renewal of our hearts, that they
may be filled with righteousness, peace, and joy in
the Holy Ghost? Let women begin this good
work; they are eminently qualified for the acceptance of the two great truths of the Gospel, love and
self-renunciation, which qualities are more or less
placed in the hearts of all women; they are naturally disposed to reverence, to worship, to self-
sacrifice, for the sake of a beloved object. These
peculiar qualities, accompanied by unenlightened
intellect and narrow views, lead them to minute
devotional practices, to the unlimited indulgence of
religious sensibility and partial unintelligent obedi-

ence. Grafted on enlightened Christianity, the
may accomplish—-what may they *not* accomplish

The women, then, who are to be the regenerator
of society, must be Christian women,—Christia
wives and Christian mothers, but enlightened Chri
tains, deeply imbued with the spirit of Christ ; no
nominal Christians, making religion (though co
soling to themselves) contemptible to those aroun
them, by their narrow and limited acceptance of i
truths. They must show forth that it is a gran
comprehensive principle, which embraces all thing
from the greatest to the least, not only our safet
but our honour, our happiness, our ultimate glor
Let them deeply engrave these principles on th
hearts of their children. It is true they cann
command results, but they will have done their di
ty. Would they be restrained by a fear of injurir
the worldly interests of their children, by the incu
cation of these unworldly principles, so little neede
for worldly advancement? Let them learn th
godliness has the promise of this world as well a
of that to come. If it be true (and the consent
ages proves it so) that happiness is not to be foun
in selfish gratification, it may be as well to seek
elsewhere. We may see how completely religic
is adapted to the nature of man, by observing th
even the elements of enjoyment (and they are man
though fleeting,) which this world contains, a
never fully tasted but by religious persons. Tho

abundant sources of pure delight which are to be found in the heart, the intellect, and the imagination, are never received in their fulness but by them; and why? because they are the germs of their future and more glorious being, and can only flourish in a soil akin to that ultimately destined for them. In a worldly mind, like plants removed from their original soil and climate, they exist, indeed, but with a blighted existence, and produce, but how degenerate is the production! Every thing that wants religion, wants vitality. Philosophy without religion is crippled and impotent; poetry without religion has no heart-stirring power; life without religion is a complex and unsatisfactory riddle; the very arts which address themselves to the senses, never proceed so far towards perfection as when employed on religious subjects. Religion, then, can be no obstacle to enjoyment, since the only sources of it which are confessedly pure, are all enhanced by its possession. Even in the ordinary commerce with the world, what a blessing awaits an exemption from the low and sordid spirit, the petty passions and paltry feelings which abound in it! The truth is, that the religious heart enjoys more keenly all that others enjoy, and has, besides, an added and superior joy of its own:

> He is the happy man, whose life e'en now
> Shows somewhat of that happier life to come.

And as to the effects of this unworldly spirit on

worldly success, it is frequently not so adverse
may be thought; but, putting aside that view of
question, let us ask what a Christian mother
consider prosperity to be but the discipline wh
may fit her children for their true and final hom
their ultimate and glorious destiny?   No effort
hers can secure to her child the good things
this world, but she may put him in possession
a principle which will add double zest to them
possessed, and supply their absence if wanting.
any other principle thus comprehensive, thus e
bracing every possible contingency of future li
How can we doubt, when we see a religion giv
to man bearing so completely the stamp of all
operations of Providence, " simplicity of princi
and universality of operation ;" once thoroug
received into the soul, it is the elixir vitæ of
securing to the possessor the certainty of pea
securing to others consistency of action, and e
biting in all things that unity of design which
the stamp of all great works, divine as well
human.

Thus all is now brought within the compass
one single principle, Christian faith,—love, s
renunciation, consistency, all the virtues rec
mended follow as necessarily from that faith
grapes from the vine, or figs from the fig-tree.
Christianity then be the basis of women's o
education—the basis of the education which t

give to their children ; so shall they perform their
mission, not with murmuring and repining at their
inferior nature and narrow sphere, but with joy and
rejoicing that they are agents in that great work,
which, if they are Christians, they daily pray for,—
that the kingdom of God may come, and his will
be done, as in heaven so on earth. May we have
strength and grace to echo this prayer, not only
with our lips, but with our lives, and to labour in
the cause as those grateful for inestimable benefits,
and conscious of their mission. That mission contains, perhaps, the destinies of society ; the wish to
accomplish it, the means of accomplishing it, should
never be out of woman's mind. Ought it then to
be excluded from her early thoughts, ought it to
be stifled by education, corrupted by worldly-
mindedness, ridiculed by folly, and checked by
opposition ? This world has nothing to offer in
exchange for such a sacrifice,—the sacrifice of the
consciousness of a high mission, and the power of
fulfiling it. It was said by an eloquent French
woman, " We are born to adorn the world, rather
than to command it." We are born for neither ;
we are born for a nobler destiny than either ; we
are born to serve it. We are made to captivate
the imagination, chiefly that we may influence the
heart of man ; and the woman who does not so
use her powers is guilty of a breach of trust worse
than that of the servant who hid his lord's talent

13

in a napkin. It is not a simple neglect, but a
abuse of his good gift, of that gift, the value an
dignity of which, man would never have known bu
for the religion of Christ. Let us then rejoice in the
liberty with which we are made free, and prove ou
love for our Lord and Master, by efforts for promo
ting his kingdom and establishing his will. And le
us work in faith and patience, nothing doubting, be
cause the result of our efforts does not always chee
and bless ourselves. This is the trial of our faith
and love. It has been the appointed trial of all
whom God has condescended to intrust with a mission. One sows that another may reap; but faith
needs not to see the harvest to know that it will
come, and that even if it do not come, no act of hum-
ble trust or fervent love is lost. But we hope more
cheering things; one cause of deficient results is
the want of comprehensiveness in principles fundamentally right. This evil will every day be reme-
died; and it highly becomes the champions of truth
to try to remedy it, or the champions of falsehood
will be too strong for them. Christians must be
not only devoted, but enlightened, if they would
meet the exigencies of the times and their own
duties. The seeds which we plant may come up,
we know not how or where, when our heads are
laid low in the dust: and souls rescued from bond-
age, and generations yet unborn, may have cause
to bless the hand that planted them!

CONCLUSION.

THE destiny of woman, as we see, is not a trifling destiny,—the mission of woman is not a trifling mission,—the influence which she possesses and exercises is not a trifling influence. Ought women then to be triflers? Ought their education and their pursuits to embrace only a round of elegant trifles? Should the cultivation of external graces form the chief object in the training of beings, so influential and responsible? Such training adds to their influence, while it takes from them the power of directing it, and increases their responsibilities without imparting the capacity requisite for their fulfilment. There is nothing so dangerous as the possession of influence undirected by conscientiousness, and it seems playing with the destinies of society to allow such powers to remain in hands so little fitted to direct them.

The influence of women is, or ought to be, a moral influence; and that it may have its full effect, the main object of their education ought to be to expand and perfect their moral nature, and to implant deeply the fact of their influence, and their own consequent responsibilities. This foundation being laid, let women be elegant, be accomplished, be every thing that society requires of them ; but let them not forget that these powers are not given for themselves, but for God's glory and the good of their fellow-creatures. Thus shall they be not only caressed, admired, honoured, but happy ; happy in the happiness of unselfishness, of devotedness, of love,—the only happiness here below which can give us any foretaste of that which is to be enjoyed above.

God grant that these truths may sink deep into women's hearts ! If this expression of them arouse a few minds to reflection and consciousness, the writer will be blessed in her work. If it induce some more powerful mind and abler pen, to do the subject greater justice, it will have accomplished much good. It is a subject of infinite importance; and it is astonishing that it should have remained almost unnoticed, in the stir and effort of society for its own renovation. Its importance is beginning now to be perceived ; its true bearings seem not always to be so. Errors are fatal on such a vital point ; and errors are especially likely to arise on a subject so interwoven with the weaknesses and frailties of our nature. The only wide view of the case, can be taken from the vantage ground of strong and enlightened Christian faith. It is our duty, therefore, to induce all whom we can influence, to view it from that point, and each in our

several places and relations to endeavour to do so.
Thus shall we fulfil our own noble mission, and
show our gratitude to Him who has done so much
for us? It is vain, through cowardly and selfish
indolence, to conceal from ourselves the fact, that
the moral destinies of the world are, in some measure, in our hands : and we must rouse ourselves
to the task, if we would not incur the condemnation of God, and of our own hearts!

THE END.

(J. P. WRIGHT, PRINTER, 18 NEW STREET.)